All we like sheep have gone astray;
we have turned every one to his own way.
And the Lord hath laid on Him
the iniquity of us all.
(Isaiah 53:6)

Nous étions tous errants comme des brebis,
nous nous sommes détournés chacun
dans son chemin.
Mais le Seigneur a pris sur Lui
toutes nos iniquités.
(Isaïe 53:6)

Wir gingen alle in der Irre wie Schafe,
wandten uns ein jeder
seines Wegs;
Jahwe aber ließ Ihn treffen
unser aller Schuld.
(Jesaja 53:6)

GEORGE FRIDERIC HANDEL (1685-1759)
MESSIAH HWV 56

ORATORIO IN THREE PARTS
FOUNDLING HOSPITAL VERSION 1754

SANDRINE PIAU SOPRANO
KATHERINE WATSON SOPRANO
ANTHEA PICHANICK CONTRALTO
RUPERT CHARLESWORTH TENOR
ANDREAS WOLF BASS-BARITONE

LE CONCERT SPIRITUEL CHOIR & ORCHESTRA
HERVÉ NIQUET CONDUCTOR

GEORGE FRIDERIC HANDEL
MESSIAH (1754)

CD1

CD2

Part III

TOTAL TIME: 69'17

SOMMAIRE | CONTENTS | INHALT

MON MESSIE
PAR HERVÉ NIQUET

Pourquoi pas un énième *Messie*, d'abord ?

Je suis allé chercher, parmi les différentes moutures qui existent du *Messie* de Haendel, la version très intéressante de 1754, à cinq solistes. Il faut savoir que lorsque Haendel arrivait dans une ville pour faire jouer son oratorio, il avait à disposition des solistes de niveau inégal. Il se dépêchait donc de remanier sa partition pour faire le déroulé de son *Messie*. Quand on se penche sur les différentes versions qui en sont nées, on remarque que des airs de soprano ont été transcrits au profit d'une alto, que tel air de basse est réduit de moitié – le chanteur devait être un peu faible. On est en prise directe avec la réalité de producteur de Haendel. C'est-à-dire qu'à l'époque, pour vivre de sa musique, le compositeur, qui ne touchait aucun droit, devait absolument faire jouer ses œuvres et engranger un bénéfice sur la soirée. L'idée de ne pas retoucher son œuvre pour ne pas l'abîmer ou la dénaturer est une idée totalement contemporaine. Il doit exister une douzaine de versions du *Messie*, je ne les ai pas toutes répertoriées ; celle de 1754 est rarement jouée parce qu'elle exige cinq solistes : deux sopranos, alto, ténor et basse.

Cette version a été enregistrée il y a trente ans par Christopher Hogwood. C'est un enregistrement que j'adore, qui m'a laissé un souvenir de propreté, d'emphase. Cet enregistrement est formidable encore aujourd'hui mais il est assez daté du point de vue organologique. On ne peut pas jouer aujourd'hui cette musique comme on le faisait sous la reine Victoria, sans toucher à rien. Je prends le parti ici d'une version opératique, modelée dans le drame qu'est cette histoire de la vie du Christ. Ce *Messie*, c'est un opéra, sacré, mais sans les soucis de la mise en scène, des décors qui n'arrivent pas, de la danseuse et du corps de ballet, des costumes pas finis. Et brusquement, on a une histoire extrêmement violente.

J'ai découvert également que le chœur avait une part dramatique extrêmement forte. Il est le sixième personnage. Dans certains airs, les cadences des solistes viennent le provoquer ; le chœur lance alors une réponse, violente. Tout s'enchaîne, dramatiquement.

J'ai aussi travaillé différemment sur la *pifa*, qui dans cette version est très courte, à peine vingt mesures. En général, elle est jouée très lentement, comme venue des anges. Je pense au contraire que ce sont les pasteurs qui arrivent et qui sont éblouis par l'ange. J'ai donc ajouté un bourdon pour avoir une musique pastorale – pas des petits moutons dans une crèche en papier. J'ai besoin ici d'entendre vraiment les bergers qui font la fête. Un vrai choc !

Donc, tout est de la main de Haendel – réorganisation, redistribution, réorchestration – mais la dramaturgie est nouvelle et vraiment impressionnante.

MY *MESSIAH*
BY HERVÉ NIQUET

First of all, why yet another *Messiah*?

I went through the different scores that exist and decided on the very interesting 1754 version, which features five soloists. You must remember that, when Handel arrived somewhere to perform his oratorio, he had soloists of varying standards available to him. So he quickly revised his score accordingly to produce a new form of his *Messiah*. When you examine the various versions that resulted, you observe that soprano arias have been transposed for alto, that a bass aria has been reduced to half its length – the singer must have been rather weak. All this is directly related to the reality of Handel's situation as a concert promoter. In those days, to earn a living from his music, a composer – who didn't receive any royalties – absolutely had to get his works performed and make a profit on the evening. The idea of not retouching a work to avoid 'spoiling' or 'distorting' it is a much more modern one. There must be around a dozen versions of *Messiah* (I won't list them all). The 1754 version is rarely performed because it calls for five soloists: two sopranos, alto, tenor and bass.

This version was recorded thirty years ago by Christopher Hogwood. It's an interpretation I love, which left me with an impression of neatness and pomp. It's still splendid today, but rather dated from an organological viewpoint. Nowadays it's no longer possible to play this music as it was done in the reign of Queen Victoria, without touching anything. I've opted here for an operatic interpretation, taking its cue from the drama inherent in this account of the life of Christ. This *Messiah* is an opera, a sacred opera, but without all the hassle of the production, the sets that don't arrive on time, the ballerina and the corps de ballet, the costumes that aren't ready. And suddenly you realise that we have an extremely violent story here.

I also discovered that the chorus has a very powerful dramatic part to play. It is the sixth character. In some of the arias, the solo cadences provoke it; then the chorus comes in with a violent response. Everything is linked, in the most dramatic fashion.

I also took a different approach to the *Pifa*, which is very short in this version, less than twenty bars. In general it's played very slowly, as if coming down from the angels. I think, on the contrary, that it represents the shepherds who arrive and are dazzled by the sight of the angel. So I added a drone to make it genuine pastoral music – not little sheep in a paper crib. I need to hear the shepherds truly rejoicing here. It makes quite an impact!

So everything here is from Handel's own pen – reorganisation, redistribution, reorchestration – but the dramaturgy is new and really impressive.

MEIN *MESSIAS*
VON HERVÉ NIQUET

Und warum eigentlich kein x-ter *Messias*?

Unter den vielen Fassungen, die es von Händels *Messias* gibt, wählte ich die sehr interessante für fünf Solisten aus dem Jahre 1754. Wenn Händel in eine Stadt kam, um sein Oratorium aufführen zu lassen, standen ihm nämlich Solisten von sehr unterschiedlichem Niveau zur Verfügung. Er beeilte sich daher, seine Partitur umzuarbeiten, um den Ablauf des *Messias* festzusetzen. Wenn man sich mit den verschiedenen, so entstandenen Fassungen auseinandersetzt, bemerkt man, dass Sopranarien für Altstimme umgeschrieben wurden oder eine bestimmte Bassarie um die Hälfte gekürzt – der Sänger war wohl nicht sonderlich gut. So steht man in direktem Bezug zur Realität des Produzenten Händel. Das heißt, dass ein Komponist in dieser Zeit, in der es keinerlei Urheberrechte gab, unbedingt seine Werke aufführen lassen und Gewinn erzielen musste, um von seiner Musik leben zu können. Die Idee, sein Werk nicht zu überarbeiten, um es nicht zu entstellen oder zu verunstalten, ist jedenfalls eine heutige Idee. Es gibt wohl ein Dutzend Fassungen des *Messias*, ich habe kein Verzeichnis davon aufgestellt; die von 1754 wird selten gespielt, weil sie fünf Solisten erfordert: zwei Soprane, Alt, Tenor und Bass.

Diese Fassung wurde vor dreißig Jahren von Christopher Hogwood aufgenommen. Ich liebe diese Aufnahme, deren Sauberkeit und Emphase mir in Erinnerung geblieben sind. Noch heute ist sie großartig, doch ist sie vom Standpunkt der Instrumentenkunde ziemlich veraltet. Man kann diese Musik heute nicht spielen, wie man es unter Königin Victoria tat, ohne etwas daran zu ändern. Ich ergreife hier die Partei einer opernartigen Fassung, die sich innerhalb des Dramas der Geschichte des Lebens Christi entfaltet. Dieser *Messias* ist eine sakrale Oper, jedoch ohne die Sorgen einer Inszenierung mit dem Bühnenbild, das noch nicht da ist, der Tänzerin oder dem Ballettkorps oder den Kostümen, die noch nicht fertig sind. Und plötzlich ergibt sich eine äußerst grausame Geschichte.

Ich habe auch entdeckt, dass der Chor eine dramatisch sehr starke Rolle spielt. Er ist die sechste Figur. In manchen Arien provozieren ihn die Kadenzen der Solisten, worauf der Chor sehr heftig antwortet. Alles reiht sich dramatisch geschickt aneinander.

Ich arbeitete auch anders an der *Pifa*, die in dieser Fassung sehr kurz ist, kaum zwanzig Takte. Im allgemeinen wird sie sehr langsam gespielt, als käme sie von den Engeln. Ich denke hingegen, dass hier die Hirten kommen und von der Erscheinung des Engels geblendet sind. Ich habe daher einen Bordun hinzugefügt, um eine pastorale Musik zu erlangen – keine kleinen Schafe in einer Papierkrippe. Ich muss hier wirklich die feiernden Hirten hören. Ein echter Schock!

Alles stammt demnach aus Händels Hand – Umorganisation, Umbesetzung, Uminstrumentierung – doch die Dramaturgie ist neu und wirklich eindrucksvoll.

GEORG FRIEDRICH HAENDEL – *LE MESSIE*
PAR PETER WOLLNY

Lorsque le « Grand Oratorio spirituel, intitulé Le Messie » de Haendel fut joué pour la première fois le 13 avril 1742 dans le Music Hall de Dublin récemment construit, plus d'un des sept cents auditeurs présents dut saisir intuitivement l'importance exceptionnelle de cette œuvre musicale. Mais nul, pas même le compositeur, ne pouvait imaginer que cette même œuvre allait devenir en peu d'années un des plus grands succès publics de tous les temps et qu'elle exercerait une influence décisive sur le développement ultérieur du genre. Alors âgé de cinquante-sept ans, Haendel se trouvait depuis plusieurs années dans une situation professionnelle précaire. Ses opéras, qui avaient rencontré autrefois un grand succès auprès du public londonien, étaient moins bien accueillis depuis que, vers le milieu des années 1730 environ, les mélodies brillantes, simples et émouvantes, des jeunes compositeurs napolitains s'étaient imposées sur les scènes concurrentes. Après qu'au cours des premiers mois de l'année 1737, trois de ses nouveaux opéras étaient tombés l'un après l'autre, même ce maestro sûr de lui-même qu'était Haendel fut forcé de constater que son étoile au ciel de l'opéra londonien commençait à décliner. La conséquence en fut une grave crise physique et psychologique dont il mit du temps à se remettre.

Une cure qu'il entreprit en septembre 1737 à Aix-la-Chapelle lui permit cependant de puiser de nouvelles forces, et lorsqu'il revint à Londres, il était de nouveau prêt à combattre pour regagner la faveur du public. Mais il était encore indécis sur la stratégie à suivre. Ce fut sans doute la commande qu'il reçut de composer une ode funèbre pour la mort de sa protectrice de longue date, la reine Charlotte, qui lui donna l'idée d'aborder le genre presque inconnu en Angleterre de l'oratorio et de lui insuffler une nouvelle vie. L'abandon de l'opéra et la décision de se consacrer durablement à l'oratorio – qui marque le début de la dernière période créatrice de Haendel – se firent progressivement : entre 1737 et 1740, il composa encore deux opéras, mais déjà quatre oratorios, dont les sujets – conformément à la tradition italienne – étaient de nature tantôt allégorique, tantôt biblique.

Le texte que son vieil ami le librettiste Charles Jennens lui proposa à l'été 1741 représentait une véritable innovation : cette présentation de la vie de Jésus ne reposait pas, comme il était usuel, sur les récits des quatre Évangiles, mais suivait en grande partie les textes des prophètes de l'Ancien Testament. Haendel semble avoir été stimulé par ce livret inhabituel dont la matière lui offrait la possibilité d'unir de manière tout à fait inédite les différentes traditions de l'opéra italien, des «anthems» anglais et des oratorios de la passion allemands. On peut mesurer son enthousiasme et l'intensité de son inspiration artistique à la durée extrêmement brève qu'il mit à composer le *Messie* : il commença cette œuvre monumentale le 22 août et la termina seulement trois semaines plus tard, le 14 septembre.

Haendel et Jennens étaient deux personnalités aux génies apparentés, liés par une relation chaleureuse, mais aussi deux caractères excentriques. Une fois que Haendel eut fini son œuvre, Jennens commença à lui suggérer de nombreuses modifications. Il avait en outre des projets très précis pour la première exécution. Son idée était de faire jouer l'oratorio sur les scènes de Londres comme un événement qui ferait sensation pendant la semaine de la Passion de 1742. Mais Haendel ne se laissa pas impressionner par l'insistance de son ami et suivit ses propres plans. Il avait ainsi accepté une invitation de William Cavendish, troisième duc de Devonshire et Lord lieutenant d'Irlande, à venir à Dublin pour y donner quelques concerts. Comme on peut le lire dans différents journaux de l'époque, il préparait déjà la création de son nouvel oratorio, *Messiah*, dans la capitale irlandaise sous forme de concert de bienfaisance au bénéfice de trois fondations charitables. Jennens dut céder.

Le succès de la création dublinoise donna raison à Haendel. L'afflux du public fut si grand qu'on put déjà vendre des billets d'entrée pour la répétition générale. Le journal *Dublin News-Letter* déclara dès après la première répétition qu'on n'avait jamais rien entendu de semblable. Et le *Dublin Journal* écrivit après la création : « Le sublime, le grand et le tendre, adaptés aux paroles les plus élevées, les plus majestueuses et les plus émouvantes, conspirèrent pour charmer et transporter les oreilles et les cœurs ravis ».

Lorsque l'œuvre fut enfin exécutée à Londres en mars 1743, les réactions furent bien plus réservées. Le public trouva d'abord étrange qu'une grande œuvre spirituelle sur la vie de Jésus soit présentée dans une salle de concert. Haendel semble avoir prévu ce problème car il avait fait omettre le titre original et annoncer son œuvre simplement comme « A new sacred oratorio ». Sans se laisser impressionner par les premières réactions hésitantes de ses auditeurs, il remit le *Messie* au programme en 1744 et 1745. La véritable carrière triomphale de l'œuvre ne commença cependant qu'avec l'exécution du 1er mai 1750, dans le cadre d'un concert de bienfaisance en faveur d'un orphelinat, le Foundling Hospital. Ayant reconnu que sa composition ne produisait tout son effet qu'avec un effectif d'une importance appropriée, Haendel accrut peu à peu le nombre des choristes et la taille de son orchestre. D'après les factures du Foundling Hospital, on comptait une soixantaine d'exécutants en 1754. Reprenant une idée antérieure – en plus de quelques autres petites modifications –, Haendel distinguait à présent dans l'effectif les *soli* des *ripieni*.

L'insistance sur l'aspect monumental s'est encore renforcée dans la seconde moitié du XVIIIe siècle. Lors des célébrations pour le centenaire de la naissance de Haendel, en juin 1784 – c'est-à-dire, par erreur, un an trop tôt –, l'exécution du *Messie* rassembla cinq cents musiciens, et lors de sa reprise, un an plus tard, ils étaient déjà plus de six cents. Ce furent ces exécutions mémorables qui inaugurèrent une redécouverte de Haendel qui se prolongea loin dans le XIXe siècle. Dans cette nouvelle forme sonore opulente, les qualités de la musique de Haendel se développaient d'une manière que l'on considéra de partout comme l'idéal de la musique spirituelle – Johann Adam Hiller parlait de l'union de « la simplicité et de la dignité », de « la grâce et de la puissance ». Joseph Haydn aurait été ému aux larmes lors d'une exécution du *Messie* : il considérait cet événement comme l'étincelle initiale de son oratorio, *La Création*. Et Ludwig van Beethoven copiait des extraits de l'œuvre pendant qu'il travaillait à sa *Missa Solemnis*. La tradition de l'oratorio au XIXe siècle est impensable sans le *Messie*.

GEORGE FRIDERIC HANDEL – *MESSIAH*
BY PETER WOLLNY

When 'Mr. *Handel's new Grand Oratorio, call'd The Messiah*' was first performed in the newly built Dublin Music Hall on 13 April 1742, not a few of the audience of around 700 must have intuitively grasped the outstanding significance of this composition. But scarcely anyone could have imagined that within a few years it would become one of the biggest popular successes of all time and would have a decisive influence on the future development of the genre – not even the composer himself. The then fifty-seven-year-old Handel had been in a precarious situation for several years. His operas, which had once been fêted by the London public, were no longer quite so popular, and since around the mid-1730s the brilliant, touching and catchy melodies of the young Neapolitan composers were increasingly heard. After three of his new operas in a row flopped in the first months of 1737, even the self-confident maestro must have noticed that his star was beginning to wane in the London operatic sky. The result was a severe physical and psychological crisis, from which he recovered only slowly.

However, a cure in Aix-la-Chapelle, taken in September 1737, allowed him to regain his strength, and on his return to London he was ready to resume the struggle for public favour. But which strategy he should pursue was not clear to him at first. It was probably the commission to compose a funeral anthem on the death of Queen Charlotte, his patron of many years, that gave him the idea of turning to the genre of the oratorio, almost unknown in England, and giving it a new lease of life. His disengagement from opera and enduring conversion to oratorio – a phase that marks the beginning of Handel's late period – occurred step by step; between 1737 and 1740 he wrote two further operas, but also four oratorios, whose subjects, following the Italian tradition, were either allegorical or biblical.

A genuine innovation came with the text that his long-time friend and librettist Charles Jennens offered Handel in the summer of 1741: an account of the life of Jesus, which was not based, as was customary, on the narratives of the four Gospels, but consisted largely of passages from the Old Testament prophets. This unusual text seems to have appealed to the composer, for the material offered him the possibility of combining traditions from the Italian opera, the English anthem and the German Passion oratorio in a completely new way. His enthusiasm and the intensity of his artistic inspiration may be judged from the blisteringly fast pace at which he wrote: Handel began the monumental composition on 22 August and finished it, after only three weeks, on 14 September.

Handel and Jennens were congenial personalities, sincerely attached to each other, but at the same time somewhat eccentric. Once the composer had finished his work, Jennens began to propose numerous changes; moreover, he also had very specific plans for the first performance. It was his wish to have the oratorio mounted as a great sensation on the London stages during Passiontide in 1742. But Handel did not let himself be swayed by the pressure from his friend, and pursued plans of his own. This entailed accepting in November

1741 an invitation from William Cavendish, Third Duke of Devonshire and Lord Lieutenant of Ireland, to travel to Dublin and give some concerts there. As may be gathered from various newspaper reports, however, he was simultaneously preparing the first performance of his new oratorio *Messiah* in the Irish capital, to be given as a benefit concert in favour of three charitable foundations. Jennens was left in the lurch.

The success of the Dublin premiere confirmed Handel's calculation. Public demand was so great that tickets were already sold for the dress rehearsal. Even after the first rehearsal, the *Dublin News-Letter* wrote that nothing comparable had ever been heard. And the *Dublin Journal* reported after the premiere: 'The Sublime, the Grand, and the Tender, adapted to the most elevated, majesty and moving Words, conspired to transport and charm the ravished Heart and Ear.'

When the work was finally performed in London in March 1743, reactions were much cooler. In the first place, the public found it strange that a large-scale sacred work on the life of Christ should be presented in a concert hall. Handel had apparently foreseen this problem, because he suppressed the original title and had the music advertised simply as 'A new sacred oratorio'. Unaffected by the initial hesitancy of his listeners, he included *Messiah* in his programmes again in 1744 and 1745. But the real triumphal progression of the work began only when it was performed on 1 May 1750 as part of a benefit concert in favour of the Foundling Hospital. For, having realised that the sublime effect of his composition was fully achieved only with correspondingly large forces, Handel gradually expanded the number of choristers and the dimensions of his orchestra. It may be inferred from the account books of the Foundling Hospital that the number of participants increased to about sixty in 1754; as a corollary to this, among other minor changes, he returned to an earlier idea and differentiated between solo and ripieno in the performing parts.

The emphasis on the monumental was amplified in the second half of the eighteenth century. For the performance of *Messiah* organised in June 1784 to mark the centenary of the composer's birth – which was mistakenly placed a year too early – 500 musicians were mobilised, and when the occasion was repeated a year later there were already more than 600. It was these memorable performances that ushered in a Handel Revival which extended far into the nineteenth century. In this new and opulent sonic guise, the characteristics of Handel's composition unfolded in a fashion that was everywhere regarded as the ideal of sacred music. Johann Adam Hiller spoke of the union of 'simplicity with dignity' and 'grace with strength'. Joseph Haydn is said to have been moved to tears after a performance of *Messiah*; he regarded this experience as the initial spark for his oratorio *The Creation*. And Ludwig van Beethoven copied out extracts from the work while he was composing the *Missa Solemnis*. The oratorio tradition of the nineteenth century is inconceivable without *Messiah*.

GEORG FRIEDRICH HÄNDEL – *MESSIAH*
VON PETER WOLLNY

Als am 13. April 1742 in der neuerbauten Dubliner Music Hall Händels „Großes Geistliches Oratorium, genannt Der Messias" erstmals aufgeführt wurde, dürfte manch einer der etwa 700 Anwesenden die überragende Bedeutung dieser Komposition intuitiv erfasst haben. Dass dieses Stück innerhalb weniger Jahre zu einem der größten Publikumserfolge aller Zeiten avancieren und die weitere Entwicklung der Gattung maßgeblich beeinflussen würde, konnte allerdings kaum jemand erahnen – nicht einmal der Komponist selbst. Der damals 57jährige Händel befand sich seit mehreren Jahren beruflich in einer prekären Lage. Seine einst vom Londoner Publikum gefeierten Opern kamen nicht mehr so recht an, seit ab etwa Mitte der 1730er Jahre auf den Konkurrenzbühnen zunehmend die brillanten, anrührenden und eingängigen Melodien der jungen neapolitanischen Komponisten erklangen. Nachdem in den ersten Monaten des Jahres 1737 nacheinander gleich drei seiner neuen Opern durchfielen, muss auch der selbstbewusste Maestro bemerkt haben, dass sein Licht am Londoner Opernhimmel zu verlöschen begann. Die Folge war eine schwere physische und psychische Krise, von der er sich nur langsam erholte.

Eine im September 1737 unternommene Kur in Aachen ließ ihn jedoch neue Kräfte schöpfen, und bei seiner Rückkehr nach London war er bereit, den Kampf um die Gunst des Publikums erneut aufzunehmen. Doch welche Strategie er dabei verfolgen sollte, war ihm zunächst nicht klar. Vermutlich war es der Auftrag, eine Trauerode auf den Tod seiner langjährigen Gönnerin Queen Charlotte zu komponieren, der ihn auf die Idee brachte, sich der in England nahezu unbekannten Gattung des Oratoriums zuzuwenden und diese mit neuem Leben zu füllen. Die Ablösung von der Oper und die dauerhafte Hinwendung zum Oratorium – eine Phase, die den Beginn von Händels später Schaffenszeit markiert – vollzog sich schrittweise; zwischen 1737 und 1740 schrieb er noch zwei Opern, aber auch bereits vier Oratorien, deren Soggetti – der italienischen Tradition folgend – teils allegorischer Natur und teils biblisch waren.

Eine echte Neuerung war der Text, den sein langjähriger Freund und Librettist Charles Jennens Händel im Sommer 1741 anbot: eine Darstellung des Lebens Jesu, die jedoch nicht, wie sonst üblich, auf den Erzählungen der vier Evangelien beruhte, sondern weitgehend den Weissagungen der alttestamentlichen Propheten folgte. Dieser ungewöhnliche Text scheint Händel gereizt zu haben, denn der Stoff bot die Möglichkeit, auf ganz neuartige Weise Traditionen der italienischen Oper, des englischen Anthem und des deutschen Passionsoratoriums zu vereinen. Seine Begeisterung und die Intensität der künstlerischen Inspiration lassen sich an der rasant kurzen Entstehungszeit messen: Händel begann mit der monumentalen Komposition am 22. August und vollendete sie nach nur drei Wochen am 14. September.

Händel und Jennens waren kongeniale, einander herzlich zugetane, zugleich aber exzentrische Persönlichkeiten. Nachdem Händel sein Werk abgeschlossen hatte, begann Jennens, zahlreiche Änderungen vorzuschlagen, außerdem hatte er ganz konkrete Pläne für die Erstaufführung. Es war sein Wunsch, das Oratorium in der Passionszeit 1742 als große Sensation auf die Londoner Bühnen zu bringen. Doch Händel ließ sich von dem Drängen seines Freundes nicht beeindrucken und verfolgte eigene Pläne. Dazu gehörte, dass er im November 1741 eine Einladung von William Cavendish, dem dritten Duke of Devonshire und Lord Lieutenant von Irland annahm, nach Dublin zu reisen und dort einige Konzerte zu geben. Wie verschiedenen Zeitungsberichten zu entnehmen ist, bereitete er gleichzeitig aber schon die Uraufführung seines neuen Oratoriums *Messiah* in der irischen Hauptstadt vor, und zwar als Wohltätigkeitskonzert zugunsten von drei karitativen Stiftungen. Jennens hatte das Nachsehen.

Der Erfolg der Dubliner Uraufführung bestätigte Händels Kalkül. Der Andrang des Publikums war so groß, dass bereits für die Generalprobe Eintrittskarten verkauft wurden. Die Zeitung *Dublin News-Letter* schrieb schon nach der ersten Probe, dass wohl niemals etwas Vergleichbares erklungen sei. Und das *Dublin Journal* berichtete nach der Premiere: „The Sublime, the Grand, and the Tender, adapted to the most elevated, majestick and moving Words, conspired to transport and charm the ravished Heart and Ear."

Als das Werk im März 1743 schließlich auch in London zur Aufführung kam, waren die Reaktionen weitaus kühler. Zunächst zeigte sich das Publikum befremdet, dass ein großes geistliches Werk über das Leben Jesu in einem Konzerthaus präsentiert wurde. Händel hatte dieses Problem offenbar vorhergesehen, denn er unterdrückte den originalen Titel und ließ die Musik schlicht als „A new sacred oratorio" ankündigen. Unbeeindruckt von der anfänglichen Zögerlichkeit seiner Zuhörer setzte er den *Messiah* auch 1744 und 1745 aufs Programm. Der eigentliche Siegeszug des Werks begann aber erst mit der Aufführung am 1. Mai 1750 im Rahmen eines Benefizkonzerts zugunsten des Foundling Hospital. Nachdem Händel nämlich erkannt hatte, dass die großartige Wirkung seiner Komposition erst mit einer entsprechend großen Besetzung zu voller Geltung kam, erweiterte er Schritt für Schritt die Zahl der Choristen und den Umfang seines Orchesters. Abrechnungen des Foundling Hospital ist zu entnehmen, dass die Zahl der Mitwirkenden im Jahr 1754 auf etwa 60 anstieg, wobei Händel – neben anderen kleineren Änderungen – eine frühere Idee wieder aufgriff und in der Besetzung zwischen Soli und Ripieni differenzierte.

Die Betonung des Monumentalen hat sich in der zweiten Hälfte des 18. Jahrhunderts noch verstärkt. Bei der im Juni 1784 veranstalteten – also irrtümlich ein Jahr zu früh angesetzten – Zentenarfeier von Händels Geburt wurden für die Aufführung des *Messias* 500 Musiker aufgeboten, bei deren Wiederholung ein Jahr später waren es bereits mehr als 600. Es waren diese denkwürdigen Aufführungen, die eine bis weit ins 19. Jahrhundert reichende Händel-Renaissance einleiteten. In dieser neuen, opulenten Klanggestalt entfalteten sich die Eigenheiten von Händels Musik auf eine Weise, die man allenthalben als das Ideal der geistlichen Musik ansah – Johann Adam Hiller sprach von der Vereinigung von „Simplicität mit Würde" und „Anmuth mit Stärke". Joseph Haydn soll nach einer Darbietung des *Messiah* zu Tränen gerührt gewesen sein; er betrachtete dieses Erlebnis als Initialzündung für sein Oratorium *Die Schöpfung*. Und Ludwig van Beethoven kopierte sich Auszüge der Komposition, während er an der Missa Solemnis arbeitete. Die Oratorientradition des 19. Jahrhunderts ist ohne den *Messias* nicht vorstellbar.

LE CONCERT SPIRITUEL
HERVÉ NIQUET

ORCHESTRA

VIOLINS I
ALICE PIÉROT (CONCERTMASTER)
FANNY PACCOUD
BÉRENGÈRE MAILLARD
MATTHIEU CAMILLERI
YANNIS ROGER

VIOLINS II
OLIVIER BRIAND
FLORENCE STROESSER
STEPHAN DUDERMEL
MYRIAM CAMBRELING
BENJAMIN CHÉNIER

VIOLAS
GÉRALDINE ROUX
MARIE-LIESSE BARAU
BENJAMIN LESCOAT

CELLOS
TORMOD DALEN (CONTINUO)
JULIE MONDOR
NILS DE DINECHIN

DOUBLE BASSES
LUC DEVANNE
BRIGITTE QUENTIN

OBOES
HÉLOÏSE GAILLARD
LUC MARCHAL
ELISABETH PASSOT

BASSOONS
JÉRÉMIE PAPASERGIO
MÉLANIE FLAHAUT
STÉPHANE TAMBY

TRUMPETS
JEAN-FRANÇOIS MADEUF
JÉRÔME PRINCE

TIMPANI
ISABELLE CORNÉLIS

HARPSICHORD
ELISABETH GEIGER (CONTINUO)

ORGAN
FRANÇOIS SAINT YVES (CONTINUO)

CHOIR

SOPRANOS
AGATHE BOUDET
GWENAËLLE CLEMINO
AUDE FENOY
ALICE GLAIE
ALICE KAMENEZKY
MÉLUSINE DE PAS
EDWIGE PARAT
INGE VAN DE KERKHOVE
MARIE-PIERRE WATTIEZ

ALTOS
JULIA BEAUMIER
MARIANNE BYLOO
DAMIEN FERRANTE
ALICE HABELLION
LUCIA NIGOHOSSIAN
YANN ROLLAND

TENORS
EDMOND HURTRAIT
MARTIAL PAULIAT
PIERRE PERNY
BENOIT PORCHEROT
PASCAL RICHARDIN
RANDOL RODRIGUEZ

BASSES
SIMON BAILLY
IGOR BOUIN
LAURENT BOURDEAUX
SYDNEY FIERRO
JEAN-CHRISTOPHE LANIÈCE
DAVID WITCZAK

HERVÉ NIQUET

TOUT À LA FOIS CLAVECINISTE, ORGANISTE, PIANISTE, CHANTEUR, COMPOSITEUR, CHEF DE CHŒUR ET CHEF D'ORCHESTRE, HERVÉ NIQUET EST L'UNE DES PERSONNALITÉS MUSICALES LES PLUS INVENTIVES DE CES DERNIÈRES ANNÉES, RECONNU NOTAMMENT COMME UN SPÉCIALISTE ÉMINENT DU RÉPERTOIRE FRANÇAIS DE L'ÈRE BAROQUE À CLAUDE DEBUSSY.

IL CRÉE LE CONCERT SPIRITUEL EN 1987 AVEC POUR AMBITION DE FAIRE REVIVRE LE GRAND MOTET FRANÇAIS. EN TRENTE ANS, LA FORMATION S'EST IMPOSÉE COMME UNE RÉFÉRENCE INCONTOURNABLE DANS L'INTERPRÉTATION DU RÉPERTOIRE BAROQUE.

DANS LE MÊME ESPRIT ET POSTULANT QU'IL N'Y A QU'*UNE* MUSIQUE FRANÇAISE SANS AUCUNE RUPTURE TOUT AU LONG DES SIÈCLES, HERVÉ NIQUET DIRIGE LES GRANDS ORCHESTRES INTERNATIONAUX AVEC LESQUELS IL EXPLORE LES RÉPERTOIRES DU XIXE SIÈCLE ET DU DÉBUT DU XXE SIÈCLE. SON ESPRIT PIONNIER DANS LA REDÉCOUVERTE DES ŒUVRES DE CETTE PÉRIODE L'AMÈNE À PARTICIPER À LA CRÉATION DU PALAZZETTO BRU ZANE — CENTRE DE MUSIQUE ROMANTIQUE FRANÇAISE À VENISE EN 2009, AVEC LEQUEL IL MÈNE À BIEN DE NOMBREUX PROJETS.

HERVÉ NIQUET EST DIRECTEUR MUSICAL DU CHŒUR DE LA RADIO FLAMANDE ET PREMIER CHEF INVITÉ DU BRUSSELS PHILHARMONIC. SOUS SA DIRECTION, CES DEUX FORMATIONS SONT TRÈS IMPLIQUÉES DANS LA COLLECTION DISCOGRAPHIQUE DES CANTATES DU PRIX DE ROME SOUS L'ÉGIDE DU PALAZZETTO BRU ZANE, AINSI QUE DES OPÉRAS INÉDITS. IL EST PAR AILLEURS DIRECTEUR ARTISTIQUE DU FESTIVAL DE L'ABBAYE DE SAINT-RIQUIER BAIE DE SOMME.

SA DÉMARCHE COMPREND AUSSI UNE GRANDE IMPLICATION PERSONNELLE DANS DES ACTIONS PÉDAGOGIQUES AUPRÈS DE JEUNES MUSICIENS (ACADÉMIE D'AMBRONAY, JEUNE ORCHESTRE DE L'ABBAYE AUX DAMES, SCHOLA CANTORUM, CONSERVATOIRE NATIONAL SUPÉRIEUR DE MUSIQUE ET DE DANSE DE LYON, MCGILL UNIVERSITY À MONTRÉAL, ETC.).

HERVÉ NIQUET EST CHEVALIER DE L'ORDRE NATIONAL DU MÉRITE ET OFFICIER DES ARTS ET LETTRES.

LE CONCERT SPIRITUEL

LE CONCERT SPIRITUEL FUT LA PREMIÈRE SOCIÉTÉ DE CONCERTS PRIVÉS EN FRANCE. FONDÉE AU XVIIIE SIÈCLE, ELLE S'ÉTEINT AVEC LA RÉVOLUTION FRANÇAISE. SON NOM EST REPRIS PAR HERVÉ NIQUET LORSQU'IL FONDE SON ENSEMBLE SUR INSTRUMENTS ANCIENS EN 1987, DANS LE BUT DE FAIRE REVIVRE LES GRANDES ŒUVRES DU RÉPERTOIRE FRANÇAIS JOUÉES À LA COUR DE VERSAILLES.

L'ENSEMBLE EST AUJOURD'HUI L'UN DES PLUS PRESTIGIEUX ORCHESTRES BAROQUES FRANÇAIS, INVITÉ CHAQUE ANNÉE AU THÉÂTRE DES CHAMPS-ÉLYSÉES, À LA PHILHARMONIE DE PARIS ET AU CHÂTEAU DE VERSAILLES AINSI QUE DANS LES PLUS GRANDES SALLES INTERNATIONALES COMME LE CONCERTGEBOUW D'AMSTERDAM, LE PALAIS DES BEAUX-ARTS DE BRUXELLES, L'OPÉRA DE TOKYO, LE BARBICAN, LE WIGMORE HALL OU LE ROYAL ALBERT HALL DE LONDRES.

À L'ORIGINE DE PROJETS AMBITIEUX ET ORIGINAUX DEPUIS SA FONDATION, L'ENSEMBLE S'EST SPÉCIALISÉ DANS L'INTERPRÉTATION DE LA MUSIQUE SACRÉE FRANÇAISE, SE CONSACRANT PARALLÈLEMENT À LA REDÉCOUVERTE D'UN PATRIMOINE LYRIQUE INJUSTEMENT TOMBÉ DANS L'OUBLI : *ANDROMAQUE* DE GRÉTRY, *CALLIRHOÉ* DE DESTOUCHES, *PROSERPINE* DE LULLY, *SÉMÉLÉ* DE MARAIS, *LE CARNAVAL DE VENISE* DE CAMPRA, *SÉMIRAMIS* DE CATEL, *LA TOISON D'OR* DE VOGEL, *LES MYSTÈRES D'ISIS* DE MOZART ET ENCORE *LES FÊTES DE L'HYMEN ET DE L'AMOUR* DE RAMEAU.

LARGEMENT RÉCOMPENSÉ POUR SES PRODUCTIONS ET ENREGISTREMENTS — EDISON AWARD, ECHO KLASSIK AWARD ET GRAND PRIX DE L'ACADÉMIE CHARLES CROS —, LE CONCERT SPIRITUEL ENREGISTRE, DEPUIS 2015, EXCLUSIVEMENT CHEZ ALPHA CLASSICS. ONT DÉJÀ PARU *DON QUICHOTTE CHEZ LA DUCHESSE* DE BOISMORTIER (DVD, COLLECTION CHÂTEAU DE VERSAILLES) ET TROIS PROGRAMMES DISCOGRAPHIQUES RÉUNISSANT LES *GLORIA* ET *MAGNIFICAT* DE VIVALDI, LES REQUIEM DE CHERUBINI ET PLANTADE ET *PERSÉE* DE LULLY (VERSION 1770).

CONCERTSPIRITUEL.COM

LE CONCERT SPIRITUEL EST SUBVENTIONNÉ PAR LE MINISTÈRE DE LA CULTURE ET DE LA COMMUNICATION ET LA VILLE DE PARIS. LE CONCERT SPIRITUEL REMERCIE LES MÉCÈNES DE SON FONDS DE DOTATION, EN PARTICULIER LE GROUPE SMA, MÉCÈNE DE LA GRANDE PRODUCTION LYRIQUE DE LA SAISON, AINSI QUE LES MÉCÈNES INDIVIDUELS DE SON « CARRÉ DES MUSES ». LE CONCERT SPIRITUEL BÉNÉFICIE DU SOUTIEN DE SES GRANDS MÉCÈNES : MÉCÉNAT MUSICAL SOCIÉTÉ GÉNÉRALE ET LA FONDATION BRU.

SANDRINE PIAU SOPRANO

RÉVÉLÉE AU PUBLIC PAR LA MUSIQUE BAROQUE AUX CÔTÉS DE WILLIAM CHRISTIE, PHILIPPE HERREWEGHE, OU ENCORE SIGISWALD KUIJKEN, SANDRINE PIAU AFFICHE UN LARGE RÉPERTOIRE, REFLÉTÉ PAR UNE ABONDANTE DISCOGRAPHIE, ET CONFIRME SA PLACE D'EXCEPTION DANS LE MONDE LYRIQUE. SUR LES SCÈNES D'OPÉRA, ELLE ALTERNE LES RÔLES BAROQUES, CLASSIQUES ET ROMANTIQUES : ALCINA, CLEOPATRA, PAMINA, MÉLISANDE, POUR NE CITER QU'EUX. ELLE SE PRODUIT AUSSI RÉGULIÈREMENT EN CONCERT ET EN RÉCITAL DANS LES PLUS GRANDES SALLES D'EUROPE ET D'AMÉRIQUE. SON DERNIER DISQUE « DESPERATE HEROINES », CONSACRÉ À MOZART A FAIT L'UNANIMITÉ DES CRITIQUES. CETTE SAISON SANDRINE PIAU SERA À PARIS, BRUXELLES, MUNICH, HAMBOURG POUR DES CONCERTS, AUX USA POUR UNE TOURNÉE DE RÉCITALS AINSI QU'AU FESTIVAL DE PENTECÔTE DE SALZBOURG DANS *ARIODANTE*. SANDRINE PIAU A ÉTÉ FAITE CHEVALIER DE L'ORDRE DES ARTS ET LETTRES EN 2006 ET ÉLUE « ARTISTE LYRIQUE DE L'ANNÉE » AUX VICTOIRES DE LA MUSIQUE 2009.

KATHERINE WATSON SOPRANO

APRÈS SES ÉTUDES AU TRINITY COLLEGE DE CAMBRIDGE, KATHERINE WATSON MÈNE UNE CARRIÈRE ACTIVE À LA FOIS EN CONCERT ET À L'OPÉRA. SES RÔLES COMPRENNENT IPHIS DANS *JEPHTHA*, DIANA DANS *ACTÉON* (W. CHRISTIE), *APOLLO E DAFNE* (J. COHEN, CARNEGIE HALL), *THEODORA* (CHRISTIE, LES ARTS FLORISSANTS),

TÉLAÏRE DANS *CASTOR ET POLLUX* (CURNYN, WIGMORE HALL), LE RÔLE-TITRE D'*ISBÉ* AU PALAIS DES ARTS DE BUDAPEST, MÉROPE DANS *PERSÉE* AVEC HERVÉ NIQUET, CLEOPATRA DANS *ALEXANDER BALUS* (CUMMINGS, FESTIVAL HAENDEL DE LONDRES), ARMÉLITE DANS *ZOROASTRE* (CURNYN, KOMISCHE OPER) ET GIUNONE DANS *IL RITORNO D'ULISSE* (HAÏM, CHAMPS-ÉLYSÉES). EN CONCERT ELLE A CHANTÉ *JAUCHZET GOTT* DE BACH ET DES AIRS DE HAENDEL AVEC L'ENGLISH CONCERT, LA *CANTATE DE NOËL* DE SCARLATTI (NORRINGTON), *SOLOMON* (MCCREESH), LA *MESSE NELSON* (BRITTEN SINFONIA, CONCERTGEBOUW), *SAMSON* (IRISH BAROQUE ORCHESTRA), RAMEAU ET HAENDEL AVEC LA BAYERISCHE RUNDFUNK, LE *MESSIE* (CONCERT SPIRITUEL, LES ARTS FLORISSANTS), *BELSHAZZAR, ACIS AND GALATEA* (FESTIVAL DE BEAUNE), ET DONNÉ DES RÉCITALS À L'OPÉRA DE LILLE AVEC SIMON LEPPER ET AU FESTIVAL DU LIED D'OXFORD AVEC SHOLTO KYNOCH. SA DISCOGRAPHIE COMPREND L'*ORATORIO DE NOËL* DE BACH (LAYTON / OAE / TRINITY COLLEGE CHOIR), ET UN ENREGISTREMENT HYPERION DE MADRIGAUX DE MONTEVERDI AVEC COHEN ET L'ENSEMBLE ARCANGELO.

ANTHEA PICHANICK CONTRALTO

APRÈS DES ÉTUDES DE VIOLON AU CONSERVATOIRE D'AIX-EN-PROVENCE, LA CONTRALTO ANTHEA PICHANICK ÉTUDIE LE CHANT À LA HAUTE ÉCOLE DE MUSIQUE DE GENÈVE PUIS AU CNSM DE LYON. ELLE ÉTUDIE ACTUELLEMENT AUPRÈS DE SUSAN MCCULLOCH À LONDRES. ELLE S'IMPOSE À L'ATTENTION DU MONDE MUSICAL EN REMPORTANT, EN 2014, LE PREMIER PRIX DU CONCOURS ANTONIO CESTI D'INNSBRUCK PUIS LE TROISIÈME PRIX DU CONCOURS DE FROVILLE. DEPUIS, ELLE EST L'INVITÉE D'ENSEMBLES TELS QUE LES ACCENTS (THIBAULT NOALLY), LE CONCERT SPIRITUEL (HERVÉ NIQUET), LE POÈME HARMONIQUE (VINCENT DUMESTRE), LES MUSICIENS DU LOUVRE (MARC MINKOWSKI) OU ACCADEMIA BIZANTINA (OTTAVIO DANTONE). ELLE COLLABORE RÉGULIÈREMENT AVEC LE CONCERT DE L'HÔTEL-DIEU. SERVANT BRILLAMMENT LES MAÎTRES DU XVIIIE SIÈCLE (VIVALDI, HAENDEL, PERGOLESI, MOZART), ELLE ABORDE ÉGALEMENT DES COMPOSITEURS TELS QUE ROSSINI. ELLE S'EST PRODUITE AU FESTIVAL D'OPÉRA BAROQUE DE BEAUNE, AU FESTIVAL DE SAINT-MICHEL, AU THÉÂTRE DES CHAMPS-ÉLYSÉES, À LA SEINE MUSICALE, À L'OPÉRA DE LYON...

RUPERT CHARLESWORTH TÉNOR

LA CARRIÈRE DE RUPERT CHARLESWORTH LE CONDUIT À TRAVERS L'EUROPE SUR DE PRESTIGIEUSES SCÈNES LYRIQUES COMME LA FENICE DE VENISE, LE THÉÂTRE DU BOLCHOÏ À MOSCOU ET LE FESTIVAL D'AIX-EN-PROVENCE. SES ENGAGEMENTS RÉCENTS COMPRENNENT JUPITER DANS *SEMELE* AU FESTIVAL HAENDEL DE LONDRES SOUS LA DIRECTION DE LAURENCE CUMMINGS ; LYSANDER DANS *A MIDSUMMER NIGHT'S DREAM*, DANS LA CÉLÈBRE MISE EN SCÈNE DE ROBERT CARSEN AU FESTIVAL D'AIX-EN-PROVENCE ; *THE FAIRY QUEEN* AU THEATER AN DER WIEN SOUS LA DIRECTION DE CHRISTOPHE ROUSSET, DANS UNE MISE EN SCÈNE DE MARIAME

CLÉMENT. CETTE AUTOMNE, IL INCARNERA LAERTES DANS LE *HAMLET* DE BRETT DEAN AVEC GLYNDEBOURNE ON TOUR. PARMI SES CONCERTS CETTE SAISON, CITONS UN GALA BERNSTEIN AVEC L'ORCHESTRE SYMPHONIQUE DE MONTRÉAL DIRIGÉ PAR KENT NAGANO ET LA *BROCKES-PASSION* SOUS LA BAGUETTE DE LAURENCE CUMMINGS AU FESTIVAL HAENDEL DE GÖTTINGEN. SA DISCOGRAPHIE COMPREND « NOCTURNES », UNE ANTHOLOGIE DE MÉLODIES FRANÇAISES AVEC EDWIGE HERCHENRODER, POUR LE LABEL OUTHERE MUSIC, ET UN DISQUE AVEC CAFÉ ZIMMERMANN D'ŒUVRES DE C.P.E BACH JAMAIS ENREGISTRÉES JUSQU'ICI, POUR LE LABEL ALPHA.

ANDREAS WOLF BARYTON-BASSE

LE JEUNE BARYTON-BASSE ALLEMAND ANDREAS WOLF A TRAVAILLÉ AVEC DES CHEFS COMME WILLIAM CHRISTIE, RENÉ JACOBS, MARCUS CREED, HELMUTH RILLING, JÉRÉMIE RHORER ET PETER DIJKSTRA, DES FORMATIONS COMME LE CHŒUR DE CHAMBRE DE LA RIAS, L'AKADEMIE FÜR ALTE MUSIK DE BERLIN, LE CHŒUR DE LA RADIO BAVAROISE, LE TEATRO ALLA SCALA, L'ORCHESTRE SYMPHONIQUE DE DÜSSELDORF ET CONCERTO KÖLN, AUX FESTIVALS DE SALZBOURG, LESSAY ET BEAUNE, AU FESTIVAL DE MUSIQUE DU RHEINGAU, AU FESTIVAL BACH DE STUTTGART ET AU FESTIVAL HAENDEL DE HALLE, ENTRE AUTRES. PARMI LES TEMPS FORTS RÉCENTS DE SA CARRIÈRE, CITONS *ARIADNE AUF NAXOS*, *CARMEN* ET *DIE GEZEICHNETEN* AU BAYERISCHE STAATSOPER DE MUNICH, LE *MESSIE* AVEC ANDREA MARCON AU KONZERTHAUS DE DORTMUND, L'*ORATORIO DE NOËL* AVEC L'ORCHESTRE SYMPHONIQUE DE GÖTEBORG ET ACCENTUS, LA *PASSION SELON SAINT MATTHIEU* AVEC TON KOOPMAN ET L'AMSTERDAM BAROQUE ORCHESTRA, GUGLIELMO DANS *COSÌ FAN TUTTE* AU TEATRO REAL, À LA MONNAIE ET AUX WIENER FESTWOCHEN, LEPORELLO (*DON GIOVANNI*), FIGARO (*LE NOZZE DI FIGARO*) ET *EL PÚBLICO* DE MAURICIO SOTELO, PAPAGENO (*DIE ZAUBERFLÖTE*) À GENÈVE, FALKE (*LA CHAUVE-SOURIS*) ET JUPITER (*PLATÉE*) À STUTTGART, ELVIRO (*SERSE*) AU THEATER AND DER WIEN ET ZOROASTRO (*ORLANDO*) AU SCOTTISH OPERA ET AU KOMISCHE OPER DE BERLIN.

SANDRINE PIAU

KATHERINE WATSON

ANTHEA PICHANICK

ANDREAS WOLF

RUPERT CHARLESWORTH

HERVÉ NIQUET

HARPSICHORDIST, ORGANIST, PIANIST, SINGER, COMPOSER, CHORAL AND ORCHESTRAL CONDUCTOR, HERVÉ NIQUET IS ONE OF THE MOST INVENTIVE MUSICAL PERSONALITIES OF RECENT YEARS. HE IS ACKNOWLEDGED, NOTABLY, AS AN EMINENT SPECIALIST IN THE FRENCH REPERTORY, FROM THE BAROQUE PERIOD TO CLAUDE DEBUSSY.

HE FOUNDED LE CONCERT SPIRITUEL IN 1987 WITH THE AIM OF REVIVING THE FRENCH *GRAND MOTET*. IN THIRTY YEARS, THE GROUP HAS BECOME A BENCHMARK FOR THE INTERPRETATION OF THE BAROQUE REPERTORY.

IN THE SAME SPIRIT, TRUE TO HIS POSTULATE THAT THERE IS ONLY *ONE* FRENCH MUSIC, WHICH RUNS ACROSS THE CENTURIES WITHOUT A BREAK, HERVÉ NIQUET CONDUCTS THE LEADING INTERNATIONAL ORCHESTRAS, WITH WHICH HE EXPLORES THE REPERTORIES OF THE LATE NINETEENTH AND EARLY TWENTIETH CENTURIES. HIS PIONEERING ZEAL IN FAVOUR OF THE REDISCOVERY OF THE WORKS OF THIS PERIOD PROMPTED HIM TO PARTICIPATE IN THE CREATION IN 2009 OF THE PALAZZETTO BRU ZANE — CENTRE DE MUSIQUE ROMANTIQUE FRANÇAISE IN VENICE, WITH WHICH HE REALISES NUMEROUS PROJECTS.

HERVÉ NIQUET IS MUSIC DIRECTOR OF THE FLEMISH RADIO CHOIR AND PRINCIPAL GUEST CONDUCTOR OF THE BRUSSELS PHILHARMONIC. UNDER HIS DIRECTION, THESE TWO FORMATIONS ARE HEAVILY INVOLVED IN THE SERIES OF RECORDINGS OF CANTATAS WRITTEN FOR THE PRIX DE ROME, RELEASED UNDER THE AUSPICES OF THE PALAZZETTO BRU ZANE, AND OF PREVIOUSLY UNRECORDED OPERAS. HE IS ALSO ARTISTIC DIRECTOR OF THE FESTIVAL DE L'ABBAYE DE SAINT-RIQUIER BAIE DE SOMME. HIS APPROACH TO HIS PROFESSION ALSO ENTAILS GREAT PERSONAL COMMITMENT TO EDUCATIONAL INITIATIVES FOR YOUNG MUSICIANS, AT THE ACADÉMIE D'AMBRONAY, JEUNE ORCHESTRE DE L'ABBAYE AUX DAMES, SCHOLA CANTORUM, CONSERVATOIRE NATIONAL SUPÉRIEUR DE MUSIQUE ET DE DANSE DE LYON AND MCGILL UNIVERSITY IN MONTREAL, AMONG OTHER INSTITUTIONS.

HERVÉ NIQUET IS A CHEVALIER DE L'ORDRE NATIONAL DU MÉRITE AND OFFICIER DES ARTS ET LETTRES.

LE CONCERT SPIRITUEL

THE CONCERT SPIRITUEL WAS THE FIRST PRIVATE CONCERT ASSOCIATION IN FRANCE. IT WAS FOUNDED IN THE EARLY EIGHTEENTH CENTURY AND DISAPPEARED AT THE TIME OF THE FRENCH REVOLUTION. HERVÉ NIQUET CHOSE TO TAKE UP ITS NAME IN 1987 WHEN HE FOUNDED HIS PERIOD-INSTRUMENT ENSEMBLE WITH THE AIM OF BREATHING NEW LIFE INTO THE GREAT WORKS OF THE FRENCH REPERTORY PERFORMED AT THE COURT OF VERSAILLES.

THE ENSEMBLE IS TODAY ONE OF THE MOST PRESTIGIOUS FRENCH BAROQUE ORCHESTRAS, INVITED TO APPEAR EACH YEAR AT THE THÉÂTRE DES CHAMPS-ÉLYSÉES, THE PHILHARMONIE DE PARIS AND VERSAILLES PALACE, AS WELL AS SUCH LEADING INTERNATIONAL VENUES AS THE AMSTERDAM CONCERTGEBOUW, THE PALAIS DES

BEAUX-ARTS IN BRUSSELS, TOKYO OPERA CITY CONCERT HALL, AND THE BARBICAN CENTRE, WIGMORE HALL AND ROYAL ALBERT HALL IN LONDON.

EVER SINCE IT WAS FORMED, THE GROUP HAS ORIGINATED AMBITIOUS AND ORIGINAL PROJECTS. IT HAS SPECIALISED IN PERFORMANCE OF FRENCH SACRED MUSIC, WHILE DEVOTING ITSELF IN PARALLEL TO THE DISCOVERY OF AN UNJUSTLY FORGOTTEN OPERATIC PATRIMONY, INCLUDING SUCH WORKS AS *ANDROMAQUE* (GRÉTRY), *CALLIRHOÉ* (DESTOUCHES), *PROSERPINE* (LULLY), *SÉMÉLÉ* (MARAIS), *LE CARNAVAL DE VENISE* (CAMPRA), *SÉMIRAMIS* (CATEL), *LA TOISON D'OR* (VOGEL), *LES MYSTÈRES D'ISIS* (MOZART) AND *LES FÊTES DE L'HYMEN ET DE L'AMOUR* (RAMEAU).

LE CONCERT SPIRITUEL HAS WON MANY AWARDS FOR ITS PRODUCTIONS AND RECORDINGS, AMONG THEM THE EDISON AWARD, THE ECHO KLASSIK AWARD AND THE GRAND PRIX DE L'ACADÉMIE CHARLES CROS. SINCE 2015 IT HAS RECORDED EXCLUSIVELY FOR ALPHA CLASSICS, WHICH HAS ALREADY RELEASED BOISMORTIER'S *DON QUICHOTTE CHEZ LA DUCHESSE* (DVD, CHÂTEAU DE VERSAILLES COLLECTION), A CD OF VIVALDI'S *GLORIA* AND *MAGNIFICAT,* THE REQUIEMS OF CHERUBINI AND PLANTADE AND LULLY'S *PERSÉE* (1770 VERSION). CONCERTSPIRITUEL.COM

LE CONCERT SPIRITUEL IS SUPPORTED BY THE MINISTÈRE DE LA CULTURE ET DE LA COMMUNICATION AND THE VILLE DE PARIS. LE CONCERT SPIRITUEL THANKS THE PATRONS WHO CONTRIBUTE TO ITS ENDOWMENT FUND, IN PARTICULAR THE GROUPE SMA, PATRON OF THE LARGE-SCALE OPERATIC PRODUCTION OF THE SEASON, AND THE INDIVIDUAL PATRONS OF ITS 'CARRÉ DES MUSES'. LE CONCERT SPIRITUEL BENEFITS FROM THE SUPPORT OF ITS TWO PRINCIPAL PATRONS: MÉCÉNAT MUSICAL SOCIÉTÉ GÉNÉRALE AND THE FONDATION BRU.

SANDRINE PIAU SOPRANO

A RENOWNED FIGURE IN THE WORLD OF BAROQUE MUSIC, FRENCH SOPRANO SANDRINE PIAU REGULARLY PERFORMS ON THE WORLD'S MOST IMPORTANT STAGES INCLUDING CARNEGIE HALL, SALLE PLEYEL, THE PARIS OPÉRA, WIGMORE HALL AND THE SALZBURG FESTIVAL AND IS INVITED BY MAJOR ORCHESTRAS SUCH AS THE BERLIN PHILHARMONIC, MUNICH PHILHARMONIC AND ORCHESTRE DE PARIS. SHE EMBRACES BOTH THE BAROQUE AND LYRIC SOPRANO REPERTOIRE, INTERPRETING A VARIETY OF ROLES INCLUDING CLEOPATRA, DONNA ANNA, PAMINA AND MÉLISANDE.

A CELEBRATED RECITAL SINGER OF BOTH FRENCH AND GERMAN REPERTOIRE, SHE PERFORMS WITH RENOWNED ACCOMPANISTS INCLUDING JOS VAN IMMERSEEL, ROGER VIGNOLES AND SUSAN MANOFF, WITH WHOM SHE IS PLANNING THEIR THIRD RECITAL ALBUM. WITH AN EXTENSIVE DISCOGRAPHY, HER LATEST CRITICALLY ACCLAIMED RELEASE IS A STUNNING SELECTION OF MOZART ARIAS TITLED 'DESPERATE HEROINES'. HIGHLIGHTS IN THE 2016/17 SEASON INCLUDED CONCERTS IN PARIS, BRUSSELS, MUNICH, HAMBURG (OPENING OF THE ELBPHILHARMONIE), A RECITAL TOUR IN THE USA AND *ARIODANTE* AT SALZBURG WHITSUN AND SUMMER FESTIVALS.

KATHERINE WATSON SOPRANO

KATHERINE WATSON IS AN ALUMNA OF TRINITY COLLEGE, CAMBRIDGE AND ENJOYS A BUSY CAREER ON BOTH THE CONCERT AND OPERATIC STAGES. ROLES INCLUDE IPHIS IN *JEPHTHA*, DIANA IN *ACTÉON* (W. CHRISTIE), DAFNE IN *APOLLO E DAFNE* (JONATHAN COHEN, CARNEGIE HALL), *THEODORA* (CHRISTIE, LES ARTS FLORISSANTS) TELAÏRE *CASTOR ET POLLUX* (CURNYN, WIGMORE HALL), TITLE ROLE *ISBÉ* AT THE PALACE OF ARTS, BUDAPEST, MÉROPE IN *PERSÉE* WITH HERVÉ NIQUET, CLEOPATRA IN *ALEXANDER BALUS* (CUMMINGS, LONDON HANDEL FESTIVAL), ARMÉLITE IN *ZOROASTRE* (CURNYN, KOMISCHE OPER) AND GIUNONE IN *IL RITORNO D'ULISSE* (HAÏM, CHAMPS-ÉLYSÉES). ON THE CONCERT STAGE PERFORMANCES INCLUDE BACH'S *JAUCHZET GOTT* AND HANDEL ARIAS WITH THE ENGLISH CONCERT, SCARLATTI'S *CHRISTMAS CANTATA* (NORRINGTON), *SOLOMON* (MCCREESH), 'NELSON' MASS (BRITTEN SINFONIA AT THE CONCERTGEBOUW), *SAMSON* (IRISH BAROQUE ORCHESTRA), RAMEAU AND HANDEL WITH THE BAYERISCHE RUNDFUNK, *MESSIAH* (LE CONCERT SPIRITUEL, LES ARTS FLORISSANTS), *BELSHAZZAR*, *ACIS AND GALATEA* (BEAUNE FESTIVAL), AND RECITALS AT OPÉRA DE LILLE WITH SIMON LEPPER AND THE OXFORD LIEDER FESTIVAL WITH SHOLTO KYNOCH. HER DISCOGRAPHY INCLUDES BACH *CHRISTMAS ORATORIO* (LAYTON/OAE/ TRINITY COLLEGE CHOIR) AND A HYPERION RECORDING OF MONTEVERDI MADRIGALS WITH COHEN AND ARCANGELO.

ANTHEA PICHANICK CONTRALTO

AFTER STUDYING THE VIOLIN AT THE AIX-EN-PROVENCE CONSERVATOIRE, THE CONTRALTO ANTHEA PICHANICK STUDIED SINGING AT THE HAUTE ÉCOLE DE MUSIQUE IN GENEVA, THEN AT THE CONSERVATOIRE NATIONAL SUPÉRIEUR DE MUSIQUE DE LYON. SHE NOW STUDIES WITH SUSAN MCCULLOCH IN LONDON. SHE ATTRACTED THE ATTENTION OF THE MUSICAL WORLD IN 2014, WHEN SHE WON FIRST PRIZE AT THE ANTONIO CESTI COMPETITION IN INNSBRUCK, FOLLOWED BY THIRD PRIZE AT THE FROVILLE COMPETITION. SINCE THEN SHE HAS BEEN INVITED TO APPEAR WITH SUCH ENSEMBLES AS LES ACCENTS (THIBAULT NOALLY), LE CONCERT SPIRITUEL (HERVÉ NIQUET), LE POÈME HARMONIQUE (VINCENT DUMESTRE), LES MUSICIENS DU LOUVRE (MARC MINKOWSKI) AND ACCADEMIA BIZANTINA (OTTAVIO DANTONE), AND WORKS REGULARLY WITH LE CONCERT DE L'HÔTEL-DIEU. WHILE BRILLIANTLY SERVING THE MASTERS OF THE EIGHTEENTH CENTURY (VIVALDI, HANDEL, PERGOLESI, MOZART), SHE ALSO PERFORMS SUCH COMPOSERS AS ROSSINI. SHE HAS APPEARED AT THE FESTIVAL D'OPÉRA BAROQUE DE BEAUNE, THE FESTIVAL DE SAINT-MICHEL, THE THÉÂTRE DES CHAMPS-ÉLYSÉES, LA SEINE MUSICALE AND THE OPÉRA DE LYON, AMONG OTHERS.

RUPERT CHARLESWORTH TENOR

RUPERT'S CAREER HAS TAKEN HIM THROUGHOUT EUROPE PERFORMING ON SUCH PRESTIGIOUS OPERATIC STAGES AS LA FENICE IN VENICE, THE BOLSHOI THEATRE IN MOSCOW AND THE FESTIVAL D'AIX-EN-PROVENCE. RECENT ENGAGEMENTS INCLUDE: JUPITER SEMELE AT THE (LONDON HANDEL FESTIVAL) CONDUCTED BY LAURENCE

CUMMINGS; LYSANDER IN ROBERT CARSEN'S ICONIC PRODUCTION OF *A MIDSUMMER NIGHT'S DREAM* (FESTIVAL D'AIX-EN-PROVENCE); *THE FAIRY QUEEN* AT THEATER AN DER WIEN UNDER THE BATON OF CHRISTOPHE ROUSSET AND DIRECTED BY MARIAME CLÉMENT. THIS AUTUMN RUPERT WILL PERFORM LAERTES IN BRETT DEAN'S *HAMLET* WITH GLYNDEBOURNE ON TOUR. CONCERT WORK FOR THIS SEASON INCLUDES; A BERNSTEIN GALA WITH ORCHESTRE SYMPHONIQUE DE MONTRÉAL CONDUCTED BY KENT NAGANO, *BROCKES-PASSION* CONDUCTED BY LAURENCE CUMMINGS AT THE HANDEL FESTIVAL IN GÖTTINGEN. RUPERT'S RECORDINGS INCLUDE 'NOCTURNES' A SELECTION OF FRENCH SONGS WITH EDWIGE HERCHENRODER FOR THE LABEL 'OUTHERE MUSIC' AND A DISC WITH CAFÉ ZIMMERMANN OF NEVER BEFORE RECORDED WORKS OF CPE BACH UNDER THE LABEL 'ALPHA'.

ANDREAS WOLF BASS-BARITONE

THE YOUNG GERMAN BASS-BARITONE ANDREAS WOLF HAS WORKED WITH CONDUCTORS SUCH AS WILLIAM CHRISTIE, RENÉ JACOBS, MARCUS CREED, HELMUTH RILLING, JÉRÉMIE RHORER AND PETER DIJKSTRA, INSTITUTIONS LIKE THE RIAS KAMMERCHOR, AKADEMIE FÜR ALTE MUSIK BERLIN, THE CHOR DES BAYERISCHEN RUNDFUNKS, THE TEATRO ALLA SCALA, THE DÜSSELDORFER SYMPHONIKER AND CONCERTO KÖLN, AND AT FESTIVALS INCLUDING SALZBURG, LESSAY AND BEAUNE, THE RHEINGAU-MUSIKFESTIVAL, BACHFEST STUTTGART AND THE HÄNDELFESTSPIELE HALLE. RECENT HIGHLIGHTS INCLUDE *ARIADNE AUF NAXOS*, *CARMEN*, *DIE GEZEICHNETEN* AND OTHER OPERAS AT THE BAYERISCHE STAATSOPER MUNICH, *MESSIAH* WITH ANDREA MARCON AT THE KONZERTHAUS DORTMUND, THE *CHRISTMAS ORATORIO* WITH THE GOTHENBURG SO AND ACCENTUS, THE *ST MATTHEW PASSION* WITH TON KOOPMAN AND THE AMSTERDAM BAROQUE ORCHESTRA, GUGLIELMO/*COSÌ FAN TUTTE* AT THE TEATRO REAL MADRID, LA MONNAIE AND THE WIENER FESTWOCHEN, LEPORELLO/*DON GIOVANNI*, FIGARO/*LE NOZZE DI FIGARO* AND *EL PÚBLICO* BY MAURICIO SOTELO, PAPAGENO/*DIE ZAUBERFLÖTE* IN GENEVA, FALKE/*DIE FLEDERMAUS* AND JUPITER/*PLATÉE* IN STUTTGART, ELVIRO/*SERSE* AT THEATER AN DER WIEN AND ZOROASTRO/*ORLANDO* AT SCOTTISH OPERA AND KOMISCHE OPER BERLIN.

HERVÉ NIQUET

HERVÉ NIQUET IST SOWOHL CEMBALIST, ORGANIST, PIANIST, SÄNGER, KOMPONIST, CHORLEITER ALS AUCH DIRIGENT. ER IST EINE DER FINDIGSTEN PERSÖNLICHKEITEN IM MUSIKLEBEN DER LETZTEN JAHRE UND WIRD BESONDERS ALS HERVORRAGENDER SPEZIALIST DES FRANZÖSISCHEN REPERTOIRES VON DER BAROCKZEIT BIS CLAUDE DEBUSSY ANERKANNT.

1987 GRÜNDET ER LE CONCERT SPIRITUEL MIT DEM EHRGEIZ, DIE GROSSE FRANZÖSISCHE MOTETTE WIEDER AUFLEBEN ZU LASSEN. IN DEN DREISSIG JAHREN SEINES BESTEHENS HAT SICH DAS ENSEMBLE ALS UNUMGÄNGLICHER ORIENTIERUNGSPUNKT FÜR DIE INTERPRETATION DES BAROCKEN REPERTOIRES DURCHGESETZT.

HERVÉ NIQUET GEHT DAVON AUS, DASS ES IM LAUFE DER JAHRHUNDERTE BRUCHLOS NUR *EINE* FRANZÖSISCHE MUSIK GIBT, UND DIRIGIERT IN DIESEM SINNE GROSSE INTERNATIONALE ORCHESTER, MIT DENEN ER DIE VERSCHIEDENEN REPERTOIRES DES 19. JH. UND DES BEGINNENDEN 20. JH. INTERPRETIERT. SEIN PIONIERGEIST BRACHTE IHN BEI DER WIEDERENTDECKUNG VON WERKEN AUS DIESER ZEIT DAZU, 2009 AN DER GRÜNDUNG DES PALAZZETTO BRU ZANE TEILZUNEHMEN, EINEM ZENTRUM FÜR FRANZÖSISCHE MUSIK DER ROMANTIK IN VENEDIG, MIT DEM ER ZAHLREICHE PROJEKTE ZUWEGE BRINGT.

HERVÉ NIQUET IST MUSIKALISCHER LEITER DES CHORS DES FLÄMISCHEN RUNDFUNKS UND ERSTER GASTDIRIGENT DER BRÜSSELER PHILHARMONIKER. UNTER SEINER LEITUNG SIND BEIDE BEI DEN CD-SAMMLUNGEN DER KANTATEN DES *PRIX DE ROME* UNTER DER SCHIRMHERRSCHAFT DES PALAZZETTO BRU ZANE EINERSEITS UND UNVERÖFFENTLICHTER OPERN ANDERERSEITS SEHR ENGAGIERT. ER IST AUSSERDEM KÜNSTLERISCHER LEITER DES FESTIVALS DER ABTEIL VON SAINT-RIQUIER BAIE DE SOMME.

HERVÉ NIQUET SETZT SICH AUCH PERSÖNLICH SEHR FÜR PÄDAGOGISCHE AKTIONEN MIT JUNGEN MUSIKERN EIN (ACADÉMIE D'AMBRONAY, JEUNE ORCHESTRE DE L'ABBAYE AUX DAMES, SCHOLA CANTORUM, CONSERVATOIRE NATIONAL SUPÉRIEUR DE MUSIQUE ET DE DANSE IN LYON, MCGILL UNIVERSITY MONTREAL USW.).

HERVÉ NIQUET ERHIELT DIE VERDIENSTORDEN *CHEVALIER DE L'ORDRE NATIONAL DU MÉRITE* UND *OFFICIER DES ARTS ET LETTRES*.

LE CONCERT SPIRITUEL

LE CONCERT SPIRITUEL WAR DIE ERSTE PRIVATE KONZERTGESELLSCHAFT IN FRANKREICH. SIE WURDE IM 18. JH. GEGRÜNDET UND ENDETE MIT DER FRANZÖSISCHEN REVOLUTION. HERVÉ NIQUET ÜBERNIMMT DIESEN NAMEN, ALS ER 1987 SEIN ENSEMBLE FÜR ALTE MUSIKINSTRUMENTE GRÜNDET, MIT DEM ZIEL, DIE GROSSEN AM HOF VON VERSAILLLES AUFGEFÜHRTEN WERKE DES FRANZÖSISCHEN REPERTOIRES WIEDER AUFLEBEN ZU LASSEN.

DAS ENSEMBLE, DAS HEUTE EINES DER RENOMMIERTESTEN BAROCKORCHESTER FRANKREICHS IST, WIRD JEDES JAHR INS THÉÂTRE DES CHAMPS-ÉLYSÉES, DIE PHILHARMONIE DE PARIS UND INS SCHLOSS VON VERSAILLES EINGELADEN, ABER AUCH IN DIE GRÖSSTEN INTERNATIONALEN KONZERTHÄUSER WIE DAS CONCERTGEBOUW

IN AMSTERDAM, DAS PALAIS DES BEAUX-ARTS IN BRÜSSEL, DIE OPER VON TOKIO, DAS BARBICAN CENTRE, DIE WIGMORE HALL ODER DIE ROYAL ALBERT HALL IN LONDON.

SEIT SEINER GRÜNDUNG DURCH HERVÉ NIQUET IM JAHRE 1987 LEITET DAS ENSEMBLE EHRGEIZIGE, ORIGINELLE PROJEKTE IN DIE WEGE UND SPEZIALISIERT SICH AUF DIE INTERPRETATION DER FRANZÖSISCHEN GEISTLICHEN MUSIK, WIDMET SICH ABER AUCH DER WIEDERENTDECKUNG EINES ZU UNRECHT IN VERGESSENHEIT GERATENEN OPERNREPERTOIRES: *ANDROMAQUE* VON GRÉTRY, *CALLIRHOÉ* VON DESTOUCHES, *PROSERPINE* VON LULLY, *SÉMÉLÉ* VON MARAIS, *LE CARNAVAL DE VENISE* VON CAMPRA, *SÉMIRAMIS* VON CATEL, *LA TOISON D'OR* VON VOGEL, *LES MYSTÈRES D'ISIS* VON MOZART ODER *LES FÊTES DE L'HYMEN ET DE L'AMOUR* VON RAMEAU.

HÄUFIG FÜR SEINE PRODUKTIONEN UND AUFNAHMEN AUSGEZEICHNET — EDISON AWARD, ECHO KLASSIK AWARD UND GRAND PRIX DE L'ACADÉMIE CHARLES CROS —, NIMMT *LE CONCERT SPIRITUEL* SEIT 2015 AUSSCHLIESSLICH BEI ALPHA CLASSICS AUF, WO BOISMORTIERS *DON QUICHOTTE CHEZ LA DUCHESSE* (DVD, REIHE CHÂTEAU DE VERSAILLES) SOWIE DREI CD-PROGRAMME MIT DEM *GLORIA* UND DEM *MAGNIFICAT* VON VIVALDI DEN REQUIEMS VON CHERUBINI UND PLANTADE SOWIE *PERSÉE* VON LULLY (FASSUNG 1770) BEREITS ERSCHIENEN SIND.

CONCERTSPIRITUEL.COM

LE CONCERT SPIRITUEL WIRD VOM FRANZÖSISCHEN MINISTERIUM FÜR KULTUR UND KOMMUNIKATION UND DER STADT PARIS SUBVENTIONIERT. LE CONCERT SPIRITUEL DANKT DEN MÄZENEN SEINES STIFTUNGSFONDS, BESONDERS DER GRUPPE SMA, DEM MÄZEN DER GROSSEN OPERNPRODUKTION DER SPIELZEIT, SOWIE DEN EINZELNEN MÄZENEN SEINES ‚CARRÉ DES MUSES'. DEM CONCERT SPIRITUEL KOMMT AUCH DIE UNTERSTÜTZUNG SEINER GROSSEN MÄZENE ZUGUTE : MÉCÉNAT MUSICAL SOCIÉTÉ GÉNÉRALE UND FONDATION BRU.

SANDRINE PIAU SOPRAN

SANDRINE PIAU WURDE VOM PUBLIKUM DURCH IHRE INTERPRETATION VON BAROCKMUSIK AN DER SEITE VON WILLIAM CHRISTIE, PHILIPPE HERREWEGHE ODER SIGISWALD KUIJKEN ENTDECKT. SIE VERFÜGT ÜBER EIN WEIT GESTECKTES REPERTOIRE, DAS VON IHRER REICHHALTIGEN DISKOGRAFIE WIDERGESPIEGELT WIRD UND IHREN RANG IM BEREICH DER OPER BESTÄTIGT. AUF DEN OPERNBÜHNEN INTERPRETIERT SIE ABWECHSELND BAROCKE, KLASSISCHE UND ROMANTISCHE ROLLEN, DARUNTER ALCINA, CLEOPATRA, PAMINA, MÉLISANDE USW. SIE TRITT AUCH REGELMÄSSIG IN DEN BEDEUTENDSTEN SÄLEN EUROPAS UND AMERIKAS IN KONZERTEN UND RECITALS AUF.

IHRE LETZTE CD, « DESPERATE HEROINES », IST MOZART GEWIDMET UND ERHIELT EINSTIMMIGES LOB VON DER KRITIK. IN DIESER SPIELZEIT WIRD SANDRINE PIAU IN PARIS, BRÜSSEL, MÜNCHEN UND HAMBURG KONZERTE GEBEN, IN DEN USA EINE RECITAL-TOURNEE MACHEN SOWIE BEI DEN SALZBURGER PFINGSTFESTSPIELEN IN *ARIODANTE* AUFTRETEN. SANDRINE PIAU ERHIELT IM JAHRE 2006 DEN VERDIENSTORDEN « CHEVALIER DE L'ORDRE DES ARTS ET LETTRES » UND WURDE 2009 BEI DEN « VICTOIRES DE LA MUSIQUE » ZUR « OPERNSÄNGERIN DES JAHRES » GEWÄHLT.

33

KATHERINE WATSON SOPRAN

KATHERINE WATSON IST ABSOLVENTIN DES TRINITY COLLEGE VON CAMBRIDGE UND MACHT SOWOHL IM KONZERTFACH ALS AUCH AUF OPERNBÜHNEN EINE EREIGNISREICHE KARRIERE. ZU IHREN ROLLEN GEHÖREN IPHIS IN *JEPHTHA*, DIANA IN *ACTÉON* (W. CHRISTIE), *APOLLO ET DAFNE* (J. COHEN, CARNEGIE HALL), *THEODORA* (CHRISTIE, LES ARTS FLORISSANTS), TÉLAÏRE IN *CASTOR ET POLLUX* (CURNYN, WIGMORE HALL), DIE TITELROLLE IN *ISBÉ* AM KUNSTPALAST VON BUDAPEST, *MÉROPE* IN *PERSÉE* MIT HERVÉ NIQUET, CLEOPATRA IN *ALEXANDER BALUS* (CUMMINGS, LONDON HANDEL FESTIVAL), ARMÉLITE IN *ZOROASTRE* (CURNYN, KOMISCHE OPER) UND GIUNONE IN *IL RITORNO D'ULISSE* (HAÏM, CHAMPS ELYSÉES). IM KONZERTFACH WAR KATHERINE WATSON IN BACHS *JAUCHZET GOTT* UND IN HÄNDEL-ARIEN MIT DEM ENGLISH CONCERT ZU HÖREN, IN SCARLATTIS *WEIHNACHTSKANTATE* (NORRINGTON), IN *SOLOMON* (MCCREESH), IN DER *NELSONMESSE* (BRITTEN SINFONIA IM CONCERTGEBOUW), IN *SAMSON* (IRISH BAROQUE ORCHESTRA), RAMEAU & HÄNDEL MIT DEM BAYERISCHEN RUNDFUNK, IM *MESSIAS* (CONCERT SPIRITUEL, LES ARTS FLORISSANTS), *BELSHAZZAR, ACIS AND GALATEA* (FESTIVAL VON BEAUNE) UND BEI RECITALS AN DER OPER VON LILLE MIT SIMON LEPPER SOWIE BEIM OXFORD LIEDER FESTIVAL MIT SHOLTO KYNOCH. IHRE DISKOGRAFIE ENTHÄLT BACHS *WEIHNACHTSORATORIUM* (LAYTON/OAE/TRINITY COLLEGE CHOIR) UND EINE AUFNAHME VON MONTEVERDI-MADRIGALEN MIT COHEN UND ARCANGELO BEI HYPERION.

ANTHEA PICHANICK ALT

NACH EINEM VIOLINSTUDIUM AM KONSERVATORIUM VON AIX-EN-PROVENCE STUDIERTE DIE ALTISTIN ANTHEA PICHANICK GESANG AN DER HAUTE ÉCOLE DE MUSIQUE VON GENF UND DANACH AM CONSERVATOIRE NATIONAL SUPÉRIEUR MUSIQUE ET DANSE IN LYON. ZURZEIT STUDIERT SIE BEI SUSAN MCCULLOCH IN LONDON. ALS SIE 2014 DEN ERSTEN PREIS DES ANTONIO-CESTI-GESANGSWETTBEWERBS IN INNSBRUCK SOWIE DEN DRITTEN PREIS BEIM CONCOURS DE FROVILLE/FRANKREICH GEWANN, WURDE DIE MUSIKSZENE AUF SIE AUFMERKSAM. SEITHER WIRD SIE VON ENSEMBLES WIE LES ACCENTS (THIBAULT NOALLY), LE CONCERT SPIRITUEL (HERVÉ NIQUET), LE POÈME HARMONIQUE (VINCENT DUMESTRE), LES MUSICIENS DU LOUVRE (MARC MINKOWSKI) ODER ACCADEMIA BIZANTINA (OTTAVIO DANTONE) EINGELADEN. SIE ARBEITET REGELMÄSSIG MIT LE CONCERT DE L'HÔTEL-DIEU ZUSAMMEN. EINERSEITS INTERPRETIERT SIE DIE MEISTER DES 18. JH. (VIVALDI, HÄNDEL, PERGOLESI, MOZART) IN BRILLANTER WEISE, ANDERERSEITS SINGT SIE AUCH WERKE VON KOMPONISTEN WIE ROSSINI. SIE TRAT BEIM FESTIVAL D'OPÉRA BAROQUE VON BEAUNE, BEIM FESTIVAL DE SAINT-MICHEL, AM THÉÂTRE DES CHAMPS-ÉLYSÉES, AN LA SEINE MUSICALE, AN DER OPER VON LYON USW. AUF.

RUPERT CHARLESWORTH TENOR

RUPERT CHARLESWORTH IST ABSOLVENT DER ROYAL ACADEMY OF MUSIC, WO ER GROSSZÜGIG VOM KARAVIOTIS-STIPENDIUM, DEM JOHN-KENNETH-ADAMS-STIPENDIUM, DER JOSEPHINE-BAKER-STIFTUNG, DER COUNTESS-OF-MUNSTER-STIFTUNG SOWIE VON MR UND MRS SOMMERVILLE UNTERSTÜTZT WURDE. ZURZEIT STUDIERT ER BEI PHILIP DOGHAN. 2013 GEWANN ER DEN HÄNDEL-GESANGSWETTBEWERB. SEINE KARRIERE FÜHRT IHN DURCH GANZ EUROPA, WO ER AN SO RENOMMIERTEN OPERNHÄUSERN WIE LA FENICE, VENEDIG UND DEM FESTIVAL D'AIX-EN-PROVENCE AUFTRITT. ZU SEINEN ROLLEN GEHÖREN DER SOLDAT IN *L'INCORONAZIONE DI POPPEA* AM THEATER AN DER WIEN, DAMON IN *ACIS AND GALATEA*, LYSANDER IN *A MIDSUMMER NIGHT'S DREAM* (AIX-EN-PROVENCE) USW. SEINE JÜNGSTEN ENGAGEMENTS BETREFFEN DIE CD-AUFNAHME EINES RECITALS VON ENGLISCHEN UND FRANZÖSISCHEN WERKEN MIT EDWIGE HERCHENRODER, HAYDNS *HARMONIEMESSE* (SCOTTISCH CHAMBER ORCHESTRA/TONU KALJUSTE), JUPITER IN *SEMELE* (LONDONER HÄNDEL FESTIVAL/CUMMINGS), MR RUSHWORTH IN JONATHAN DOVES *MANSFIELD PARK* SOWIE WEITERE AUFFÜHRUNGEN IN AMSTERDAM, PARIS UND LISSABON.

ANDREAS WOLF BASSBARITON

DER JUNGE DEUTSCHE BASSBARITON ANDREAS WOLF ARBEITET MIT DIRIGENTEN WIE WILLIAM CHRISTIE, RENÉ JACOBS, MARCUS CREED, HELMUTH RILLING, JÉRÉMIE RHORER UND PETER DIJKSTRA, MIT VERANSTALTERN WIE DEM RIAS KAMMERCHOR, DER AKADEMIE FÜR ALTE MUSIK BERLIN, DEM CHOR DES BAYERISCHEN RUNDFUNKS, DEM TEATRO ALLA SCALA, DEN DÜSSELDORFER SYMPHONIKERN UND DEM CONCERTO KÖLN BEI DEN SALZBURGER FESTSPIELEN, DEN FESTIVALS IN LESSAY UND BEAUNE, DEM RHEINGAU-MUSIKFESTIVAL, DEM BACHFEST STUTTGART UND DEN HÄNDELFESTSPIELEN HALLE U.A. ZU DEN HÖHEPUNKTEN DER LETZTEN ZEIT GEHÖREN *ARIADNE AUF NAXOS, CARMEN, DIE GEZEICHNETEN* USW. AN DER BAYERISCHEN STAATSOPER MÜNCHEN, DER *MESSIAH* MIT ANDREA MARCON AM KONZERTHAUS DORTMUND, DAS *WEIHNACHTSORATORIUM* MIT DEM GOTHENBURG S.O. & ACCENTUS, DIE *MATTHÄUS-PASSION* MIT TON KOOPMAN & DEM AMSTERDAM BAROQUE ORCHESTRA SOWIE FOLGENDE ROLLEN: GUGLIELMO/*COSI FAN TUTTE* AM TEATRO REAL, AN LA MONNAIE UND BEI DEN WIENER FESTWOCHEN, LEPORELLO/*DON GIOVANNI*, FIGARO/*LE NOZZE DI FIGARO* UND *EL PÚBLICO VON MARICIO SOTELO*, PAPAGENO/*DIE ZAUBERFLÖTE* IN GENF, FALKE/*DIE FLEDERMAUS* UND JUPITER/*PLATÉE* IN STUTTGART, ELVIRO/*SERSE* AM THEATER AN DER WIEN UND ZOROASTRO/*ORLANDO* AN DER SCOTTISH OPERA UND DER KOMISCHEN OPER BERLIN.

GEORGE FRIDERIC HANDEL
MESSIAH HWV 56

ORATORIO IN THREE PARTS
FOUNDLING HOSPITAL VERSION 1754

GEORGE FRIDERIC HANDEL
MESSIAH (1754)

CD1

1.

PART I
No.1 SINFONIA
Grave-Allegro moderato

2.

No.2 ACCOMPAGNATO (Tenor)
Comfort ye my people,
saith your God.
Speak ye comfortably to Jerusalem,
and cry unto her, that her warfare is accomplished,
that her iniquity is pardoned.
The voice of him that crieth in the wilderness;
Prepare ye the way of the Lord;
make straight in the desert
a highway for our God.
(Isaiah 40:1-3)

3.

No.3 AIR (Tenor)
Every valley shall be exalted,
and every moutain and hill made low;
the crooked straight and the rough places plain.
(Isaiah 40:4)

4.

No.4 CHORUS
And the glory of the Lord shall be revealed,
and all flesh shall see it together:
for the mouth of the Lord hath spoken it.
(Isaiah 40:5)

5.

No.5 ACCOMPAGNATO (Bass)
Thus saith the Lord of hosts:
Yet once a little while and I will shake
the heavens and the earth,
the sea and the dry land.
And I will shake all nations;
and the desire of all nations shall come.
(Haggai 2:6-7)

The Lord, whom ye seek,
shall suddenly come to His temple,
even the messenger of the Covenant,
whom ye delight in;
behold, He shall come,
saith the Lord of hosts.
(Malachi 3:1)

6.

No.6 AIR (Soprano)
But who may abide the day of His coming,
and who shall stand when He appeareth?
For He is like a refiner's fire.
(Malachi 3:2)

PREMIÈRE PARTIE
N° 1. SYMPHONIE
Grave-Allegro moderato

N°2. ACCOMPAGNATO (Ténor)
Consolez mon peuple,
a dit votre Dieu.
Parlez au cœur de Jérusalem,
et annoncez-lui que sa servitude est achevée,
et son injustice pardonnée.
Écoutez la voix de celui qui crie dans le désert ;
Frayez le chemin du Seigneur ;
et aplanissez dans le désert
une voie pour notre Dieu.
(Isaïe 40:1-3)

N° 3. AIR (Ténor)
Que toute vallée soit relevée,
toute montagne et toute colline abaissée ;
que le tortueux devienne droit et le rugueux lisse.
(Isaïe 40:4)

N° 4. CHŒUR.
Alors la gloire du Seigneur se révèlera,
et toute la chair la verra en même temps :
car la bouche du Seigneur a parlé.
(Isaïe 40:5)

N° 5. ACCOMPAGNATO (Basse)
Car voici que le Seigneur des armées dit :
Bientôt encore une fois j'ébranlerai
le ciel et la terre,
la mer et les continents.
Et j'ébranlerai toutes les nations ;
et le désir viendra de toutes les nations.
(Aggée 2:6-7)

Le Seigneur que vous recherchez,
viendra alors dans Son temple,
et l'ange de la nouvelle alliance,
que vous désirez aussi ;
le voici, Il va venir,
a dit le Dieu des armées.
(Malachie 3:1)

N° 6. AIR (Soprano)
Mais qui pourra supporter le jour de Sa venue,
et qui pourra demeurer debout quand Il apparaîtra ?
Car Il enflammera comme le feu du purificateur.
(Malachie 3:2)

7.

No.7 CHORUS
And he shall purify the sons of Levi,
that they may offer unto the Lord
an offering in righteousness.
(Malachi 3:3)

No.8 RECITATIVE (Contralto)
Behold, a virgin shall conceive
and bear a son
and shall call his name Emmanuel,
God with us.
(Isaiah 7:14; Matthew 1:23)

8.

No.9 AIR (Contralto) & CHORUS
O thou that tellest good tidings to Zion,
get thee up into the high mountain.
O thou that tellest good tidings to Jerusalem,
lift up thy voice with strength;
lift it up, be not afraid;
say unto the cities of Judah,
behold your God!
(Isaiah 40:9)

O thou that tellest good tidings to Zion,
Arise, shine, for thy Light is come,
and the glory of the Lord
is risen upon thee.
(Isaiah 60:1)

9.

No.10 RECITATIVE (Bass)
For behold, darkness shall cover the earth,
and gross darkness the people;
but the Lord shall arise upon thee,
and His glory shall be seen upon thee.
And the Gentiles shall come to thy light,
and kings to the brightness of thy rising.
(Isaiah 60:2-3)

10.

No.11 AIR (Bass)
The people that walked in darkness
have seen a great light;
and they that dwell in the land
of the shadow of death,
upon them hath the light shined.
(Isaiah 9:1)

11.

No.12 CHORUS
For unto us a Child is born,
unto us a Son is given:
and the government shall be
upon His shoulder;

N° 7. CHŒUR
Et Il purifiera les enfants de Lévi,
afin qu'ils puissent faire au Seigneur
leurs offrandes dans la justice.
(Malachie 3:3)

N° 8. RÉCITATIF (Contralto)
Voici, une vierge sera enceinte
et enfantera un fils
et lui donnera le nom d'Emmanuel,
Dieu soit avec nous.
(Isaïe 7:14 ; Matthieu 1:23)

N° 9. AIR (Contralto) ET CHŒUR
Ô toi qui apportes à Sion la bonne nouvelle,
monte sur une haute montagne.
Ô toi qui apportes à Jérusalem la bonne nouvelle,
élève puissamment la voix ;
crie bien haut et ne crains rien ;
et dis aux villes de Judas,
voici notre Dieu !
(Isaïe 40:9)

Ô toi qui apportes à Sion la bonne nouvelle,
Lève-toi, rayonne, car la lumière est proche,
et la gloire de Dieu
est levée sur toi.
(Isaïe 60:1)

N° 10. RÉCITATIF (Basse)
Car regarde, le ténèbres couvriront la terre,
et une nuit obscure tous les peuples ;
mais le Seigneur resplendit sur toi,
et Sa gloire apparaîtra sur toi.
Et les gentils marcheront vers ta lumière,
et les rois vers l'éclat de ton apparition.
(Isaïe 60:2-3)

N° 11. AIR (Basse)
Le peuple qui marchait dans les ténèbres
a vu une grande lumière ;
et la lumière resplendit
sur ceux qui vivaient,
au pays de l'ombre et de la mort.
(Isaïe 9:2)

N° 12. CHŒUR
Car un enfant nous est né,
un fils nous est donné :
la souveraineté sera
sur Ses épaules,

and His name shall be called
Wonderful, Counsellor, the Mighty God,
the Everlasting Father, the Prince of Peace.
(Isaiah 9:5)

et Son nom signifiera
Merveilleux, Conseiller, Dieu fort,
Père Éternel, le Prince de la Paix.
(Isaïe 9:6)

12. No.13 PIFA (Sinfonia Pastorale)

N° 13. PIFA (Symphonie pastorale)

No.14 RECITATIVE (Soprano)
There were shepherds abiding in the field,
keeping watch over their flocks by night.
(Luke 2:8)

N° 14 ; RÉCITATIF (Soprano)
Il y avait des bergers couchant dans les champs,
qui veillaient la nuit sur leurs troupeaux.
(Luc 2:8)

13. No.14b RECITATIVE (Soprano)
And lo, the angel of the Lord came upon them,
and the glory of the Lord
shone round about them,
and they were sore afraid.
(Luke 2:9)

N° 14b ; RÉCITATIF (Soprano)
Et alors l'ange du Seigneur,
et la gloire du seigneur
les illumina,
et il furent saisis d'une grande frayeur.
(Luc 2:9)

No.15 RECITATIVE (Soprano)
And the angel said unto them : Fear not,
for behold, I bring you good tidings of great joy,
which shall be to all people.
For unto you is born this day
in the city of David
a Saviour, which is Christ the Lord.
(Luke 2:10-11)

N° 15. RÉCITATIF (Soprano)
Et l'ange leur dit : ne craignez rien,
car je vous annonce une grande joie,
qui sera celle de tous les peuples.
Aujourd'hui vous est né
dans la ville de David
un sauveur qui est le Christ Seigneur.
(Luc 2:10-11)

14. No.16 ACCOMPAGNATO (Soprano)
And suddenly there was with the angel,
a multitude of the heavenly host,
praising God, and saying:
(Luke 2:13)

N° 16. ACCOMPAGNATO (Soprano)
Et aussitôt une multitude de la troupe céleste,
fut avec l'ange,
qui loua Dieu et dit :
(Luc 2:13)

15. No.17 CHORUS
Glory to God in the highest,
and peace on earth,
good will towards men.
(Luke 2:14)

N° 17. CHŒUR
Gloire à Dieu au plus haut,
et paix sur la terre,
aux hommes de bonne volonté.
(Luc 2:14)

16. No.18 AIR (Soprano)
Rejoice greatly, O daughter of Zion;
shout, O daughter of Jerusalem!
Behold, thy King cometh unto thee;
He is the righteous Saviour,
and He shall speak peace unto the heathen.
(Zachariah 9:9-10)

N° 18. AIR (Soprano)
Réjouis-toi fort, ô fille de Sion ;
crie, ô fille de Jérusalem !
Regarde, voici venir ton roi ;
Il est le juste Sauveur,
et parlera de paix à tous les peuples.
(Zacharie 9:9-10)

No.19 RECITATIVE (Soprano)
Then shall the eyes of the blind be opened,
and the ears of the deaf unstopped.
Then shall the lame man leap as an hart,
and the tongue of the dumb shall sing.
(Isaiah 35:5-6)

N° 19. RÉCITATIF (Soprano)
Alors les yeux des aveugles seront ouverts,
et les oreilles des sourds entendront.
Alors le paralytique bondira comme un cerf,
et la langue des muets chantera.
(Isaïe 35:5-6)

17.

No.20 DUET (Sopranos)
He shall feed His flock like a shepherd;
and He shall gather the lambs with His arm,
and carry them in His bosom,
and gently lead those that are with young.
(Isaiah 40:11)

Come unto Him, all ye that labour,
come unto Him that are heavy laden,
and He will give you rest.
Take His yoke upon you, and learn of Him,
for He is meek and lowly of heart,
and ye shall find rest unto your souls.
(Matthew 11:28-29)

N°20. DUO (Sopranos)
Il nourrira son troupeau, semblable au berger ;
et rassemblera doucement ses brebis dans ses bras,
il les portera en son sein,
et conduira lentement les mères avec leurs petits.
(Isaïe 40:11)

Venez à lui, vous qui peinez,
et êtes chargés lourdement de tristesse,
car Il vous soulagera.
Prenez Son joug et devenez Ses disciples,
car il a le cœur doux et humble,
vous trouverez ainsi la paix de l'âme.
(Matthieu 11:28-29)

18.

No.21 CHORUS
His yoke is easy, His burthen is light.
(Matthew 11:30)

N° 21. CHŒUR
Son joug est doux, Son fardeau est léger.
(Matthieu 11:30)

CD2

PART II

DEUXIÈME PARTIE

1.

No.22 CHORUS
Behold the lamb of God,
that taketh away the sin of the world.
(John 1:29)

N° 22. CHŒUR
Voici l'agneau de Dieu,
Qui éloigne le péché du monde.
(Jean 1:29)

2.

No.23 AIR (Contralto)
He was despised and rejected of men,
a man of sorrows
and acquainted with grief.
(Isaiah 53:3)

He gave His back to the smiters,
and His cheeks to them
that plucked off the hair:
He hid not His face
from shame and spitting.
(Isaiah 50:6)

N° 23. AIR (Contralto)
Il était dédaigné et méprisé de tous,
un homme de douleurs
et habitué à la souffrance.
(Isaïe 53:3)

Il offrait Son dos à ceux qui le frappaient,
Ses joues à ceux
qui lui arrachaient la barbe:
Il ne dérobait pas Son visage
à l'ignominie et aux crachats.
(Isaïe 50:6)

3.

No.24 CHORUS
Surely He hath borne our griefs,
and carried our sorrows!
He was wounded for our transgressions,
He was bruised for our iniquities;
the chastisement of our peace
was upon Him.
(Isaiah 53:4-5)

N° 24. CHŒUR
Sûrement Il était pour nos souffrances,
et supportait nos peines !
Il était blessé de nos péchés,
et broyé de nos iniquités ;
le châtiment qui nous apporte la paix
est tombé sur Lui.
(Isaïe 53:4-5)

4.

No.25 CHORUS
And with His stripes we are healed.
(Isaiah 53:5)

N° 25. CHŒUR
Par Ses blessures nous sommes guéris.
(Isaïe 53:5)

5.

No.26 CHORUS
All we like sheep have gone astray;
we have turned every one to his own way.
And the Lord hath laid on Him
the iniquity of us all.
(Isaiah 53:6)

N° 26. CHŒUR
Nous étions tous errants comme des brebis,
nous nous sommes détournés chacun dans son chemin.
Mais le Seigneur a pris sur Lui
toutes nos iniquités.
(Isaïe 53:6)

6.

No.27 ACCOMPAGNATO (Tenor)
All they that see Him
laugh Him to scorn;
they shoot out their lips,
and shake their heads, saying:
(Psalm 22:7)

N° 27. ACCOMPAGNATO (Ténor)
Tous ceux qui Le voient
se rient de Lui ;
ils lui font la moue,
et hochent la tête en disant :
(Psaume 22:7)

7.

No.28 CHORUS
He trusted in God that He would deliver Him;
Let Him deliver Him, if He delight in Him.
(Psalm 22:9)

N° 28. CHŒUR
Il a fait confiance à Dieu pour qu'Il le délivre :
Qu'Il le sauve, s'Il l'aime.
(Psaume 22:8)

8.

No.29 RECITATIVE (Tenor)
Thy rebuke hath broken His heart:
He is full of heaviness.
He looked for some to have pity on Him,
but there was no man,
neither found He any to comfort Him.
(Psalm 69:21)

N° 29. RÉCITATIF (Ténor)
Cette opprobre a brisé Son cœur :
Il est rempli de tristesse.
Il a cherché si quelqu'un avait de la compassion,
mais il n'y avait personne,
ni quelqu'un pour le consoler.
(Psaume 69:20)

9.

No.30 AIR (Tenor)
Behold, and see if there be any sorrow
like unto His sorrow
(Lamentations 1:12)

N° 30. AIR (Ténor)
Voyez et regardez s'il est une douleur
semblable à la douleur qui l'accable ?
(Lamentations 1:12)

10.

No.31 RECITATIVE (Soprano)
He was cut off out of the land of the living:
for the transgressions of Thy people
was He stricken.
(Isaiah 52:8)

N° 31. RÉCITATIF (Soprano)
Il était arraché à la terre des vivants :
Il était frappé
à cause des péchés de son peuple.
(Isaïe 52:8)

11.

No.32 AIR (Soprano)
But Thou didst not leave His soul in hell;
nor didst Thou suffer Thy Holy One
to see corruption.
(Psalm 16:10)

N° 32. AIR (Soprano)
Mais tu n'as point laissé Son âme au tombeau ;
et tu ne lui as pas permis
de voir la corruption.
(Psaume 16:10)

12.

No.33 CHORUS
Lift up your heads, O ye gates;
and be ye lift up, ye everlasting doors;
and the King of Glory shall come in.
Who is this King of Glory?
The Lord strong and mighty,
The Lord mighty in battle.
Who is this King of Glory?

N° 33. CHŒUR
Rehaussez-vous, ô portes éternelles,
Et ouvrez-vous tout grand ;
Que le Roi de gloire fasse son entrée.
Quel est ce Roi de Gloire ?
C'est le Seigneur fort et tout-puissant ,
le Seigneur puissant dans la bataille.
Quel est ce Roi de Gloire ?

The Lord of Hosts,
He is the King of Glory.
(Psalm 24:7-10)

No.34 RECITATIVE (Tenor)
Unto which of the angels
said He at any time:
Thou art My Son,
this day have I begotten Thee?
(Hebrews 1:5)

13. **No.35 CHORUS**
Let all the angels of God worship Him.
(Hebrews 1:6)

14. **No.36 AIR (Soprano)**
Thou art gone up on high;
Thou hast led captivity captive,
and received gifts for men;
yea, even from Thine enemies,
that the Lord God might dwell among them.
(Psalm 68:18)

15. **No.37 CHORUS**
The Lord gave the word;
great was the company of the preachers.
(Psalm 68:12)

16. **No.38 AIR (Soprano)**
How beautiful are the feet of them
that preach the gospel of peace,
and bring glad tidings of good things.
(Isaiah 52:7 / Romans 10:15)

17. **No.39 CHORUS**
Their sound is gone out into all lands,
and their words unto the ends of the world.
(Romans 10:18)

18. **No.40 AIR (Bass)**
Why do the nations so furiously rage together,
and why do the people imagine a vain thing?
The kings of the earth rise up,
and the rulers take counsel together
against the Lord,
and against His Anointed.
(Psalm 2:1-2)

19. **No.41 CHORUS**
Let us break their bonds asunder,
and cast away their yokes from us.
(Psalm 2:3)

No.42 RECITATIVE (Tenor)
He that dwelleth in heaven
shall laugh them to scorn;
the Lord shall have them in derision.
(Psalm 2:4)

C'est le Seigneur des armées,
Il est le Roi de Gloire.
(Psaume 24:7-10)

N° 34. RÉCITATIF (Ténor)
Auquel des anges
a-t-il jamais dit :
Tu es Mon Fils,
ce jour je t'ai engendré ?
(Hébreux 1:5)

N° 35. CHŒUR
Que tous les anges de Dieu l'adorent.
(Hébreux 1:6)

N° 36. AIR (Soprano)
Tu es monté dans les airs ;
Tu as amené des prisonniers captifs,
Et reçu des dons pour ces hommes ;
Et même pour tes ennemis,
Afin que le Dieu Tout-puissant demeure parmi eux.
(Psaume 68:18)

N° 37. CHŒUR
Le Seigneur leur donna la parole ;
Les prêcheurs étaient en foule innombrable.
(Psaume 68:12)

N° 38. AIR (Soprano)
Qu'ils sont beaux les pieds de celui
qui publie la paix,
qui apporte de bonnes nouvelles.
(Isaïe 52:7 / Romains 10:15)

N° 39. CHŒUR
Leur voix est sortie dans toutes les terres,
et leurs paroles jusqu'aux extrémités du monde.
(Romains 10:18)

N° 40 AIR. (Basse)
Pourquoi les nations s'assemblent-elles en fureur,
   pourquoi les peuples préparent-ils de vains complots ?
Les rois de la terre se sont levés,
et les princes ont tenu conseil ensemble
contre le Seigneur,
et contre son Oint.
(Psaume 2:1-2)

N° 41. CHŒUR
Debout, brisons leurs chaînes,
et rejetons loin de nous leurs liens.
(Psaume 2:3)

N° 42. RÉCITATIF (Ténor)
Celui qui trône dans les cieux
Se rira de leur colère ;
Le Seigneur les tournera en dérision.
(Psaume 2:4)

20. No.43 AIR (Tenor)
Thou shalt break them with a rod of iron;
Thou shalt dash them in pieces
like a potter's vessel.
(Psalm 2:9)

21. No. 44 CHORUS
Hallelujah: For the Lord God Omnipotent reigneth.
(Revelation 19:6)
The Kingdom of this world
is become the Kingdom of our Lord,
and of His Christ;
and He shall reign for ever and ever.
(Revelation 11:15)
King of Kings, and Lord of Lords.
(Revelation 19:16)
Hallelujah!

PART III

22. No.45 AIR (Soprano)
I know that my Redeemer liveth,
and that He shall stand
at the latter day upon the earth.
And though worms destroy this body,
yet in my flesh shall I see God.
(Job 19:25-26)

For now is Christ risen from the dead,
the first fruits of them that sleep.
(I Corinthians 15:20)

23. No.46 CHORUS
Since by man came death,
by man came also
the resurrection of the dead.
For as in Adam all die,
even so in Christ
shall all be made alive.
(I Corinthians 15:21-22)

24. No.47 RECITATIVE (Bass)
Behold, I tell you a mystery;
we shall not all sleep,
but we shall all be changed
in a moment,
in the twinkling of an eye, at the last trumpet.
(I Corinthians 15:51-52)

25. No.48 AIR (Bass)
The trumpet shall sound,
and the dead shall be raised incorruptible,
and we shall be changed.
(I Corinthians 15:52-53)

N° 43. AIR (Ténor)
Tu les briseras avec une barre de fer,
Tu les mettras en pièces
Comme un vase de potier.
(Psaume 2:9)

N° 44. CHŒUR
Alléluia : car le Seigneur Tout-puissant règne.
(Révélations 19:6)
Le Royaume du monde
est désormais le royaume du Seigneur,
et de Son Christ ;
et Il règnera pour toujours.
(Révélations 11:15)
Roi des rois, Dieu des dieux,
(Révélations 19:16)
Alléluia !

TROISIÈME PARTIE

N° 45. AIR (Soprano)
Je sais que mon Rédempteur vit,
et qu'Il restera
jusqu'au dernier jour de la terre.
Et bien que les vers auront détruit mon corps,
je verrai encore Dieu dans ma chair.
(Job 19:25-26)

Car Christ est ressuscité,
prémices pour ceux qui dorment.
(I Corinthiens 15:20)

N° 46. CHŒUR
Car puisque la mort venue par un homme,
c'est aussi par un homme
qu'est venue la résurrection des morts.
De même que tous meurent en Adam,
tous revivront
dans le Christ.
(I Corinthiens 15:21-22)

N° 47. RÉCITATIF (Basse)
Voici, je vous dévoile un mystère :
nous ne mourrons pas tous,
mais tous nous seront changés
en un instant,
en un clin d'œil, à la trompette dernière.
(I Corinthiens 15:51-52)

N° 48. AIR (Basse)
La trompette sonnera,
et les morts ressusciteront incorruptibles
et nous serons changés.
(I Corinthiens 15:52-53)

No.49 RECITATIVE (Contralto)
Then shall be brought to pass
the saying that is written:
Death is swallowed up in victory.
(I Corinthians 15:54)

N° 49. RÉCITATIF (Contralto)
Alors sera accompli
ce qui est écrit :
la Mort a été engloutie dans la victoire.
(I Corinthiens 15:54)

26. **No.50 DUET (Contralto / Tenor)**
O death, where is thy sting?
O grave, where is thy victory?
The sting of death is sin,
and the strength of sin is the law.
(I Corinthians 15:55-56)

N° 50. DUO (Contralto/Ténor)
Ô Mort, où est ton dard ?
Ô tombeau, où est ta victoire ?
Le dard de la mort c'est le péché,
et la puissance du péché c'est la Loi.
(I Corinthiens 15:55-56)

27. **No.51 CHORUS**
But thanks be to God
who giveth us the victory
through our Lord Jesus-Christ.
(I Corinthians 15:57)

N° 51. CHŒUR
Mais grâces soient rendues à Dieu
qui nous a donné la victoire
par notre Seigneur Jésus-Christ.
(I Corinthiens 15:57)

28. **No.52 AIR (Soprano)**
If God be for us,
who can be against us?
(Romans 8:31)

N° 52. AIR (Soprano)
Si Dieu est avec nous,
qui peut être contre nous ?
(Romains 8:31)

Who shall lay anything
to the charge of God's elect?
It is God that justifieth,
who is he that condemneth?
It is Christ that died,
yea rather, that is risen again,
who is at the right hand of God,
who makes intercession for us.
(Romans 8:33-34)

Qui pourra dire quelque chose
contre l'élu de Dieu ?
Si Dieu est celui qui justifie,
quel est celui qui condamnera ?
C'est le Christ qui est mort,
et qui de plus est ressuscité,
Il est assis à la main droite de Dieu,
et intercède pour nous.
(Romains 8:33-34)

29. **No.53 CHORUS**
Worthy is the Lamb
that was slain,
and hath redeemed us
to God by His blood,
to receive power, and riches, and wisdom,
and strength, and honour,
and glory and blessing.
Blessing and honour, glory and power,
be unto Him
that sitteth upon the throne,
and unto the Lamb,
for ever and ever.
Amen.
(Revelations 5:12-14)

N° 53. CHŒUR
Gloire à l'Agneau
Qui a été tué,
et nous a réconciliés
avec Dieu par son sang,
pour recevoir force et richesse et sagesse,
et puissance et honneur,
et gloire et grandeur et grâce.
Nous Lui devons
puissance et honneur et gloire,
Lui qui siège sur le trône,
ainsi que l'Agneau,
pour toujours et toujours.
Amen.
(Révélations 5:12-14)

VOUS AIMEZ LA MUSIQUE
NOUS SOUTENONS CEUX QUI LA FONT

MÉCÉNAT MUSICAL SOCIÉTÉ GÉNÉRALE
GRAND MÉCÈNE DU CONCERT SPIRITUEL

FONDATION BRU

AU SERVICE DE GRANDES CAUSES, LA FONDATION BRU OFFRE AUX TALENTS ET AUX BELLES INITIATIVES, LES MOYENS D'ALLER DE L'AVANT, POUR CHANGER DURABLEMENT LES CHOSES. CRÉÉE À L'INITIATIVE DU DOCTEUR NICOLE BRU AFIN DE PÉRENNISER LA MÉMOIRE DES CRÉATEURS DES LABORATOIRES UPSA, ELLE SOUTIENT ET ACCOMPAGNE DANS LA DURÉE DES PROJETS INNOVANTS, BIEN CONÇUS, PORTÉS PAR UNE VISION À LONG TERME... LES RENDANT PARFOIS TOUT SIMPLEMENT POSSIBLES.

ENGAGÉE, PROFONDÉMENT HUMANISTE, PIONNIÈRE, À L'IMAGE DE LA FAMILLE DE CHERCHEURS ENTREPRENEURS DONT ELLE PORTE LE NOM, LA FONDATION BRU PLACE L'HOMME AU CŒUR DE SES ACTIONS ET INTERVIENT DANS DES DOMAINES TRÈS VARIÉS.

PAR SON MÉCÉNAT CULTUREL, LA FONDATION BRU CONTRIBUE À LA SAUVEGARDE DE PATRIMOINES, FAVORISE LA DIFFUSION DES CONNAISSANCES ET L'ÉMERGENCE DE NOUVEAUX TALENTS ET FAIT PARTAGER DES ÉMOTIONS.

PARMI SES ENGAGEMENTS EN FAVEUR DE LA MUSIQUE :
- LE CONCERT SPIRITUEL
LES DOCTEURS JEAN ET NICOLE BRU ONT ASSURÉ UN SOUTIEN INDÉFECTIBLE À HERVÉ NIQUET DÈS 1987. LA FONDATION BRU A PRIS LE RELAIS, POUR CONTRIBUER AU RAYONNEMENT DE LA MUSIQUE BAROQUE EN EUROPE ET DANS LE MONDE.
- LE PALAZZETTO BRU ZANE – CENTRE DE MUSIQUE ROMANTIQUE FRANÇAISE
CETTE FONDATION ŒUVRE, DEPUIS VENISE, À LA REDÉCOUVERTE DU PATRIMOINE MUSICAL FRANÇAIS DU GRAND XIXE SIÈCLE.

Créé en 2014, le fonds de dotation du Concert Spirituel, sous la présidence de Jean-Jacques Aillagon, permet aux entreprises et particuliers d'accompagner Le Concert Spirituel dans son développement. Les dons collectés assurent le rayonnement de l'ensemble en France et dans le monde, au service du patrimoine musical français, à travers des productions prestigieuses.
Outil de soutien indispensable à la redécouverte de chefs-d'œuvre inédits, il permet également à d'enthousiasmantes actions culturelles menées auprès de collégiens d'exister.

Le Concert Spirituel remercie les mécènes de son fonds de dotation, en particulier le groupe SMA, mécène de la grande production lyrique de la saison, ainsi que les mécènes individuels de son Carré des Muses.

concertspirituel.com

RECORDED FROM 20 TO 22 DECEMBER 2016 AT NOTRE-DAME DU LIBAN (PARIS)
MANUEL MOHINO RECORDING PRODUCER, EDITING & MASTERING

CHARLES JOHNSTON ENGLISH TRANSLATION
SILVIA BERUTTI-RONELT GERMAN TRANSLATION
LAURENT CANTAGREL FRENCH TRANSLATION
VALÉRIE LAGARDE DESIGN & ARTWORK

COVER IMAGE: © PLAINPICTURE/LP/SCOTT GORDON

INSIDE PHOTOS: LE BON PASTEUR, ANONYME PORTUGAIS.
© RMN-GRAND PALAIS (MUSÉE DE LA RENAISSANCE, CHÂTEAU D'ECOUEN) / MATHIEU RABEAU (P.2)

© LE CONCERT SPIRITUEL (P.12-13) © JULIEN MIGNOT (HERVÉ NIQUET P.21) © SANDRINE EXPILLY (SANDRINE PIAU P.26)
© HUGO BERNAND (KATHERINE WATSON P.26) © JAVIER DEL REAL (ANDREAS WOLF P.27)
© JULIEN CHERKI (ANTHEA PICHANICK P.27) © GERARD COLLETT (RUPERT CHARLESWORTH P.27)

"LE PATICIER", NICOLAS II DE LARMESSIN (1632/38–1694) © AKG-IMAGES (P.54)
UNE CUISINIÈRE / LE CONFISEUR / LA CONFISEUSE, MARTIN ENGELBRECHT (1684-1756)
©PHOTO JOSSE/LEEMAGE (P.68, P.84 & 101)

ALPHA CLASSICS
DIDIER MARTIN DIRECTOR
LOUISE BUREL PRODUCTION
AMÉLIE BOCCON-GIBOD EDITORIAL COORDINATOR

LE CONCERT SPIRITUEL
42, RUE DU LOUVRE
F-75001 PARIS
PHONE +33(0)1 40 26 11 31
CONCERTSPIRITUEL .COM

AUDE MASSIET DU BIEST DIRECTOR
CLÉO BLASSEL PRODUCTION
ÉMILIE-CHARLOTTE FRANÇOIS COMMUNICATION AND PARTNERSHIP
MARIE-CAPUCINE GUILLOCHON FUNDRAISING
MYRIAM KOUNDOUNO ADMINISTRATION
ISABELLE PICHON-VARIN PRODUCTION
JULIANA RICHARD BOOKING

PRINTED IN MALAYSIA BY TIEN WAH PRESS

49

LE MiLLe Feuille
D'HERVÉ NIQUET

LE MiLLeFeuiLLe

D'HERVÉ NIQUET

Hervé Niquet ouvre son arrière-cuisine avec ce millefeuille superposant souvenirs, humeurs, coups de gueule et passions, spécialement dressé pour les trente ans du Concert Spirituel. À déguster avec gourmandise.

Chef de chœur, chef d'orchestre, fondateur du Concert Spirituel, grand amoureux de la musique française, baroque mais pas que, défricheur de partitions des Prix de Rome avec le Palazzetto Bru Zane, comédien loufoque dans les mises en scène d'opéra de ses amis Shirley et Dino, amateur de jardinage et de San-Antonio père, passionné d'architecture, chroniqueur déjanté et matinal sur France Musique, inconditionnel picard et directeur artistique du Festival de Saint-Riquier… Hervé Niquet ne se prend pas au sérieux et néanmoins fait sérieusement ce qu'il a à faire. C'est un drôle d'humaniste, ou un humaniste drôle, qui aime ses musiciens – et ses musiciens le lui rendent bien. Lui qui n'hésite pas à mettre la main à la pâte, qui salive à l'idée de mitonner des petits plats pour ses amis et montre une admiration respectueuse envers les chefs cuisiniers comme Bernard Pacaud ouvre son arrière-cuisine avec ce millefeuille superposant souvenirs, humeurs, coups de gueule et passions, spécialement dressé pour les trente ans du Concert Spirituel. À déguster avec gourmandise.

BONNES SŒURS

« J'ai beaucoup appris auprès des bonnes sœurs qui ont fait mon éducation à Abbeville : l'architecture – on vivait dans un lieu bâti entre le XVe et le XVIIIe siècle –, l'orgue, la musique… Tout le monde était dans la même blouse, et je peux vous dire que ça ouvre l'imaginaire d'avoir un uniforme ! J'y ai suivi toute ma scolarité, de la maternelle jusqu'au bac, pour tout un tas de raisons qui se complétaient.

Je ne réfléchis même plus à comment les choses se sont enchaînées mais ça s'est fait tout naturellement : j'ai changé de professeur de piano, qui était la directrice de la chorale paroissiale et qui m'a envoyé à Amiens ; j'ai chanté dans la chorale, j'ai tenu l'orgue puis j'ai dirigé la chorale. C'est toujours comme ça dans les paroisses : l'un pousse l'autre. Et puis on s'essaie à ses premières compositions, alors on prend un cours d'harmonie, puis de contrepoint. On se rend compte que c'est utile et très simple si ça sert dès le lendemain à quelque chose. C'est très excitant parce que c'est toujours collé à une réalité scénique, théâtrale. J'en ai écrit des messes et des cantiques et des machins comme ça ! C'est ça l'apprentissage. »

PIANO

« Ma mère avait décidé de me mettre au piano, idée d'ascension sociale sans doute. Mon père avait rapporté un instrument à la maison, arrivé dans une bétaillère, sorti d'une ferme et acheté 10 francs. Comme je m'ennuyais un peu avec mes professeurs, mon père m'achetait des partitions au kilo chez un brocanteur, tous ces ouvrages qu'il y avait dans les bonnes maisons bourgeoises. Alors vous lisez avec deux doigts toutes les opérettes, toutes les symphonies de Beethoven réduites – *La Cocarde de Mimi-Pinson*, qui connaît ça ? Moi, ça me faisait rire, et j'ai lu comme ça tout Mozart, Mendelssohn, Haydn, Wagner… Comme j'avais horreur du sport, je lisais de la musique, tout ce qui me passait sous les doigts ! C'est comme ça que je me suis fait ma littérature, tout seul – et je ne l'ai pas regretté un instant, quand je suis arrivé à vingt ans à l'Opéra de Paris, de pouvoir déchiffrer n'importe quoi à n'importe quelle heure. »

MAURICE RAVEL

« Jeune, je n'ai pas eu accès à grand-chose. Lorsque je suis allé faire mes études de piano à Amiens, vers quatorze ou quinze ans, j'ai eu pour professeur Marie-Cécile Morin, une copine de classe de Samson François chez Marguerite Long. Quand elle avait elle-même douze ans et qu'elle travaillait les pièces de Ravel, Marguerite Long lui disait : "Travaille bien tes pièces, au prochain cours, je demanderai à Maurice de passer." Maurice *Ravel* ! Et elle revenait avec sa petite partition, Éditions Leduc, je m'en souviens encore, et elle jouait avec Ravel à côté d'elle, qui la corrigeait, lui notait les phrasés, les doigtés et lui disait ce à quoi il fallait penser. Et quand moi je travaillais Ravel avec elle, elle me disait :

"La semaine prochaine j'apporterai ma partition." Sa partition *annotée par Ravel*. Pour moi, ça a été le premier contact avec les sources originales. Le coup de crayon rouge, le petit mot en bas de page, le petit sourire, le petit dessin étaient de la main de Maurice Ravel ! Pour moi, il appartenait à l'histoire, aux livres, pas à la réalité. Ça a été un choc. Lorsque plus tard, une fois entré à l'Opéra de Paris, j'ai rencontré Madeleine Milhaud qui me racontait son mari, Satie, Colette ou Cocteau, quand Serge Lifar me racontait Bakst, Diaghilev ou Picasso, j'étais comme dans un livre d'histoire. »

DÉCLIC

« Quand j'avais quinze ans, le violoniste Pierre Amoyal est venu dans ma campagne faire un concert avec sa femme et une claveciniste. Celle-ci avait un instrument moderne des années 1960, qui même jeté du quatrième étage marche encore, impeccable, avec cinq pédales, le crochet pour le chien, une étagère pour les casseroles, et qui s'éclaire à l'intérieur… Bref, j'ai été fasciné par cet instrument que je ne comprenais pas, que je n'avais jamais vu. Je suis *tombé par terre* ! C'était la première fois que j'entendais du Bach ou du Rameau joué sur un clavecin. Je suis rentré à la maison et j'ai demandé à ma grand-mère – je m'étais renseigné – de me prêter des sous : "Mémé, je voudrais m'acheter un kit de clavecin. Je voudrais avoir un instrument comme ça." J'ai abandonné tous les Beethoven, les Brahms, les Chopin, et j'ai plongé mon nez dans tout ce que j'avais comme partitions – évidemment modernes – de Rameau et compagnie pour essayer de comprendre. Je suis allé à Paris voir le facteur de clavecins Marc Ducornet ; je lui ai acheté un petit kit, que j'ai commencé à monter avec un ami. J'ai construit cinq, six, sept clavecins, que j'ai revendus par la suite. Je voulais essayer de comprendre pourquoi ça marchait comme ça. Ce concert a été le déclic. J'ai fait la jonction avec la musique sacrée, que j'avais pratiquée comme organiste à la chorale paroissiale, et j'ai commencé à plonger un peu le nez dans les disques.

Aujourd'hui, ça me fait tout drôle de rejouer du clavecin. Je l'ai fait récemment à Bruges pour remplacer le continuiste de *Don Quichotte chez la Duchesse*. Je me suis retrouvé quarante ans en arrière ! Ça m'a amusé, et ça a amusé les musiciens. Mais je ne fais plus ça. Il y en a qui font ça mille fois mieux que moi. »

DANSE

« À l'origine, je suis venu à Paris parce que je voulais être danseur. J'avais quelques facilités : je sautais bien, je tournais bien, j'étais souple. J'avais commencé à Abbeville, poursuivi au conservatoire d'Amiens, fait trois mois de Conservatoire de Paris, et puis stop. L'idée de devoir arrêter son métier à quarante ans parce qu'on devient vieux m'a fichu le cafard. Et puis lorsqu'on est danseur, on l'est vingt-quatre heures sur vingt-quatre. Il faut s'occuper de son corps et de sa souplesse tout le temps, pendant toute sa vie. Moi j'adorais lire, me cultiver, chercher, et ce que j'avais frôlé avec ma professeur de piano – les manuscrits – commençait à me titiller. J'ai donc arrêté la danse, et la danse y a beaucoup gagné ! Pour payer mes cours, j'accompagnais d'autres cours de danse. Noëlla Pontois, danseuse étoile à l'Opéra de Paris il y a quarante ans, m'avait repéré dans un cours à Paris et proposé de faire quelques remplacements d'accompagnateur. De fil en aiguille, et après un concours, je suis entré comme pianiste à l'Opéra de Paris pour le ballet. J'ai fait ensuite un peu de chœur, de la scène ; je me suis fait ma place dans la maison.

J'ai appris l'exigence à l'Opéra de Paris. Je suis passé de mes études à un travail professionnel avec les meilleurs chorégraphes du monde, les meilleurs danseurs du monde. Avoir comme patron Noureev ! Je n'ai pas eu de temps d'adaptation, mais cet apprentissage terrible, à vitesse grand V, m'a forgé. Ça reste un moment *extrêmement* fort de ma vie.

Aujourd'hui, la danse me sert à ne pas être étriqué dans ma direction. Je suis un peu délié, j'ai des grands bras et je n'ai pas peur de les ouvrir. Je bouge, je marche, oui. Et puis beaucoup de choses ont trait à la danse en musique. Je trouve beaucoup de solutions musicales grâce à la danse. Et pour accompagner, n'en parlons pas. »

BNF « Nous étions dans les années 1970, en plein début du renouveau baroque, avec Christopher Hogwood, Gustav Leonhardt et Jean-Claude Malgoire, René Jacobs, Philippe Herreweghe. J'allais assister aux cours pour auditeurs libres que donnait William Christie dans des petites pièces au Conservatoire. C'était très confidentiel : dans un couloir, au fin fond d'un studio de danse ou dans un entresol, on installait un clavecin, on se disposait autour et on lisait des cantates et des vieux trucs. William Christie a eu sa classe après. Il était incontournable – c'était un tel puits de science, il était tellement sûr de lui, il avait *tout* lu !

J'étais bien évidemment fasciné non seulement parce qu'il avait une réponse à tout mais parce que justement, à l'inverse des chefs de symphonique que je voyais à l'Opéra, il parlait rhétorique, figuralisme, histoire, musicologie, organologie, recherches scientifiques, autographe, manuscrits ! J'arrivais de ma province, où le seul fonds musical était celui du curé et des religieuses de l'école, et là, à Paris, pour 7 francs, je pouvais avoir un laissez-passer à la Bibliothèque nationale de France et accéder aux manuscrits de Campra et de tant d'autres ! Je me souviens encore du contact de la chaise dans la salle de lecture au cinquième étage, la première fois, je n'en revenais pas ! J'avais vingt ans et j'y allais toutes les semaines, des journées entières. Une vraie addiction !

William Christie et Nikolaus Harnoncourt – les deux que j'allais écouter – avaient des réponses parce qu'ils avaient non pas *appris* mais *cherché*. Ils étaient à l'époque parmi les seuls à savoir ce qu'ils savaient parce qu'ils avaient eux-mêmes cherché. Et quand ils n'avaient pas le temps de chercher, ils nous envoyaient chercher pour eux. C'est ce qui m'a donné le goût de cette chasse au trésor perpétuelle. »

FOUS DINGUES

« Il y a quarante ans, tout était à faire pour redécouvrir les répertoires anciens. Il reste encore aujourd'hui des musicologues fous dingues de recherche fondamentale, allumés de passion, qui apportent des solutions qu'on ne connaissait pas il y a trente, vingt ou même dix ans. Et il y a de jeunes ensembles qui vont chercher du répertoire, qui adoptent un autre comportement – parce qu'on est de plus en plus naturel là-dedans. Que de fraîcheur !

Avouons qu'on a de la chance d'avoir à la direction artistique du Centre de musique baroque de Versailles un fou royal et puits de science en la personne de Benoît Dratwicki. Sans lui, bon nombre de pans du répertoire français seraient encore à l'abandon.

Trente ans après la création du Concert Spirituel, je continue à prendre le risque de mettre des œuvres inconnues dans mes programmes. Avant, j'allais dans toutes les directions parce que j'avais un appétit pour tout. Et puis l'âge avançant, il faut canaliser l'énergie ; je vais de plus en plus vers ce que sont mes goûts. Si je fais Benevolo, c'est par goût pour la polyphonie inconnue italienne ; si je fais beaucoup de XIXe-XXe, c'est en souvenir de mes années à l'Opéra de Paris. Avec le Palazzetto Bru Zane et le Centre de musique baroque de Versailles, j'ai à mes côtés deux institutions très solides bardées de chercheurs qui m'apportent du répertoire selon mes goûts parce qu'ils me connaissent. »

VALISES

« Mon job, c'est de comprendre l'œuvre, d'avoir une vision et d'avoir à disposition des ouvriers spécialisés – les musiciens – qui peuvent réaliser les idées. Je dois arriver en répétition avec mes valises pleines de choses à transmettre – que ce soit au Concert Spirituel, au Brussels Philharmonic, à Lisbonne ou à Budapest. Chaque projet est *vraiment* important et mérite tout le travail que l'on fournit. Un musicien n'a pas fait quinze ans d'études individuelles, passé sa jeunesse à ne pas aller au sport, fait des heures et des heures de gammes, passé des concours pour s'emmerder une fois qu'il est musicien dans la vie ! Il va s'ennuyer si le chef n'est pas à la hauteur – culturelle, sociale, humaniste voire musicale. Dès lors que vous ouvrez la boîte à outils pour parler musicologie, compréhension, rhétorique, c'est le bonheur ! Dès que quelqu'un *apporte* quelque chose, même de la contradiction, de l'inattendu, fruit d'une recherche, d'une intelligence, le débat est ouvert, cela apporte forcément un autre éclairage à la vie des musiciens. Quand je dis "vie", c'est vraiment leur vie parce que l'instrument et la musique, les musiciens en font six ou dix heures par jour. Un chef ne peut pas sous-estimer l'engagement, le travail ni l'énergie que cela demande. Un orchestre n'est pas un outil : ce sont des gens. »

CARRIÈRE

« Je ne suis pas spécialement fier de ma carrière. Je ressens plus de bonheur que de fierté. Encore maintenant, quand je rentre, rue de Madrid, dans ce qui était le Conservatoire de Paris lorsque j'avais vingt ans – où je n'ai *jamais* été accepté malgré tous les concours que j'ai passés –, je ressens quelque chose de douloureux. Quand j'étais à l'Opéra de Paris, les relations entre les musiciens de l'Opéra, les chefs de chant de l'Opéra et les professeurs du Conservatoire étaient nombreuses. On m'a donc demandé d'écrire des épreuves pour les étudiants du Conservatoire, les épreuves d'entrée, les concours de lecture, les variations… alors qu'on n'avait jamais voulu de moi ! Ce complexe me pousse non pas à *prouver* mais à *chercher*. Je ne me trouve jamais assez instruit, c'est ce qui m'incite à toujours me remettre au travail. »

TROUPE

« À l'Opéra de Paris, j'ai appris à vivre dans une maison, à faire partie d'une troupe, donc quand je rentre dans une maison d'opéra, je connais très vite tout le monde – le régisseur général, l'accessoiriste, la costumière, l'habilleuse principale, le cintrier, l'éclairagiste, et les prénoms de tous… C'est tellement plus rapide, efficace, sain et simple de s'adresser ensuite aux bonnes personnes par leur prénom ! Il y a tous ces gens qui sont derrière et qui passent leur vie dans le théâtre, jamais valorisés, toujours dans le noir – et pourtant ce sont des artistes, qui nous permettent d'être, nous, dans la lumière. *Chacun* est important. *Chaque place* est importante ! Et de là naît l'harmonie, et s'il y a harmonie, il y a justesse, rythme, tout ce qu'il faut pour faire naître ce qui est écrit sur une partition. S'il y a harmonie, il y a tout – mais pour cela chacun doit être à sa place et la considérer comme essentielle. »

BRAZZAVILLE

« Si on n'est pas connecté à la réalité, si un artiste n'est pas connecté à la vie, c'est un branleur ! J'ai beaucoup été en Afrique, notamment au Congo – sous le régime de Mobutu : je m'étais lié d'amitié avec ce qui restait d'un conservatoire à Brazzaville. Avec une chanteuse et un guitariste – moi au clavier –, on était allés rencontrer des professeurs pendant quinze jours ; on avait travaillé, joué pour eux. Ils n'avaient pas un crayon, pas un bout de papier. Pendant des années, par l'intermédiaire de l'ambassade, je leur ai envoyé des kilos de papier, des kilos de crayons. Et puis un jour, le paquet m'est revenu : il n'y avait plus de conservatoire, ils avaient tous été tués. Ces gens-là ont été tués parce qu'ils essayaient d'apprendre un art non conforme à l'idée de la dictature en place. Alors il est sûr que maintenant, je ne supporte plus qu'un musicien en face de moi ne soit pas concentré à 100 % en répétition ou en concert. J'ai encore dans les yeux les visages de tous ces amis morts à cause de la musique… »

METTEURS EN SCÈNE
« J'ai eu de très bonnes expériences avec des metteurs en scène, notamment avec Christoph Marthaler, Romeo Castellucci, Shirley et Dino bien sûr. Ces quatre-là sont des gens extrêmement cultivés, qui bossent énormément. Ils ont des manières de pratiquer différentes mais ils adorent le travail. Par exemple, Christoph Marthaler : tout est prêt dans sa tête, mais il ne sait pas ce qu'il va faire. On vit cinq semaines ensemble, on monte l'opéra ensemble, on ne sait pas où on va, mais ça fonctionne le jour du spectacle. Romeo, lui, est un illustrateur et un imagier extraordinaire, c'est-à-dire qu'il vous emmène dans son livre de contes. C'est *Alice au pays des merveilles*, vous n'en croyez pas vos yeux. Et Gilles et Corinne, ils connaissent Racine, Corneille et Molière sur le bout des doigts, ils savent régir une troupe, et tout est prêt au moment où on débarque pour travailler. J'ai beaucoup aimé aussi travailler avec Mariame Clément. C'est quelqu'un d'hyper préparé, de très ouvert, qui rend poétique le moindre changement de décors et qui respecte la moindre personne.

Rien n'est jamais simple, et quand il y a des difficultés, il faut bien faire avec. Si j'accepte une production, il faut que j'aille au bout – et puis il faut protéger les gens que vous avez engagés. On vit parfois des expériences qui ne sont pas géniales mais pour lesquelles on réussit tout de même à faire quelque chose. Et puis diriger une production lyrique, c'est gérer beaucoup de soucis. On doit être prêt à sauver toutes les situations, à ne pas mettre les artistes en péril sur le plateau. »

SHIRLEY & DINO
« J'ai découvert le sens de la scène avec Corinne et Gilles Benizio – c'est finalement assez récent –, mais j'ai surtout découvert qu'il s'agissait d'un métier extrêmement difficile. Quel boulot ! Mais une fois que c'est fait, c'est formidable. Avant, je me prenais très au sérieux quand je faisais de la tragédie, mais quand j'ai vu la difficulté de faire du comique !!! Dans une tragédie, les ficelles sont très claires. Dans le comique, il faut avoir l'esprit vif, et surtout il faut être mathématicien pour réagir à la demi-seconde près. L'à-peu-près ne marche pas : il faut avoir une haute idée du rythme, être exigeant pour les autres et pour soi-même.

Avec Gilles et Corinne, on partage les mêmes goûts pour les mêmes choses parce qu'on est de la même génération. On a assisté aux débuts de la télévision, on a été admiratifs de *La Piste aux étoiles*, des Branquignols… On rit des mêmes choses et on aime le travail bien fait. Eux comme moi ne sommes pas nés sur un tas d'argent, on a ramé pour avoir ce qu'on a. On a toujours su se débrouiller avec deux bouts de ficelle, et ça ne nous fait pas peur. Coco adore cuisiner, moi aussi. Gilles adore manger. Moi je suis nul en vins, il est très fort. Il aime la moto, moi je déteste ça. On est devenus de grands amis, et nos enfants aussi. Mais au départ, c'est parce qu'il y avait beaucoup d'affinités dans le travail. »

LE CONCERT SPIRITUEL

« Le fait de créer sa propre boutique – comme je l'ai fait avec Le Concert Spirituel –, avec ses propres forces, où chaque centime est important, aller soi-même chercher les gens, monter les concerts et réussir à monter un programme, faire soi-même à la main des éditions parce qu'on a peu de moyens – j'ai fait tout le matériel d'orchestre des trente premiers disques, un boulot colossal –, ça forge le caractère. Je sais le prix de tout ça. Fonder une équipe de copains qui fonctionne depuis trente ans, c'est quelque chose !

Aujourd'hui, c'est une très belle communauté qui peut réagir d'elle-même de façon harmonieuse. C'est une éducation de trente ans. Pour faire un son, au Concert Spirituel, j'avais autrefois besoin d'un service, maintenant il me faut dix minutes. Quand de nouveaux musiciens arrivent, les collègues qui sont là les prennent en main très rapidement pour les insérer dans notre tissu. Je trouve ça très joli. Et à l'inverse de certains ensembles qui mettent les petits nouveaux dans les fonds de pupitre ou à des postes peu dangereux, nous, on les met en première ligne, assis à côté du premier violon. Ils ne sont pas là pour remplir les rangs ! C'est assez gratifiant pour eux, et on est presque toujours récompensés de ce risque que l'on prend – c'est réjouissant. »

ANGES GARDIENS

« Ils ont cru en moi et à mes projets les plus fous, contre vents et marées ! Sans eux, je ne serais pas là… Jean et Nicole Bru évidemment, la rencontre la plus importante de ma vie ! Avec Le Concert Spirituel et la Fondation Bru qui a créé le Palazzetto Bru Zane-Centre de Musique Romantique Française à Venise, Nicole Bru a sauvé plus de trois siècles de musique française. Cela mérite plus qu'une médaille, je ne sais pas, une place réservée au Panthéon ? Martine Tridde et la Fondation BNP Paribas ont été aussi des partenaires formidables, au Canada puis avec Le Concert Spirituel, pendant des années ! Désormais, j'ai la très grande chance d'être soutenu par Mécénat Musical Société Générale, grand mécène du Concert Spirituel, et par le Groupe SMA. Fait peu étonnant, les décideurs culturels de ces sociétés sont des gens cultivés, mélomanes, curieux, visionnaires, et pour certains musiciens amateurs discrets et passionnés. Le ministère de la Culture et la Mairie de Paris soutiennent également fidèlement notre aventure musicale.»

SOUS

« Dans la musique, il faut toujours aller chercher de l'argent. Deux choses vont de pair, qui sont celles pour lesquelles je fais ce métier : *primo* manger, et *secundo* rencontrer les gens. Pour ne parler que du Concert Spirituel, je fais travailler deux cents à deux cent cinquante personnes par an, selon les années. En faisant une moyenne à raison d'une famille pour un employé, cela fait mille personnes. Si je ferme la boutique, ces gens-là sont dans la peine. Si on ne pense pas aux sous qu'on rentre et aux sous qui sortent, on n'existe plus. Un euro, c'est vraiment un euro. À chaque fois que je monte sur scène, c'est une somme d'argent qui est dépensée. Donc on ne peut pas se tromper : il faut lire les partitions et être sûr de son coup. On ne va pas monter un truc sur scène où on risque tous de sombrer corps et âme.

L'artiste dans sa tour d'ivoire, c'est un mythe. Ou alors il est fabuleusement riche – ça existe, mais on voit ce que ça donne. Non, moi j'ai charge d'âmes. Il faut que tout le monde soit bon et disponible parce que sans ça, la musique ne sera pas bonne. Pour en revenir au *secundo*, la musique n'est qu'un alibi pour rencontrer les gens. Je me rends compte que là où nous avons, tous, les musiciens et moi, le plus de plaisir, c'est pendant les répétitions. Faire un beau concert, réussir à rendre tout ce qu'on a engrangé comme intelligence en répétition, c'est la cerise sur le gâteau. »

PALACE

« Un concert de chef d'orchestre sans musiciens, c'est rien. Ça n'existe pas ! Je dois faire en sorte que chaque instrumentiste ou chanteur prenne sa juste place. Car c'est dans cet échange qu'il se passe des choses. Le Concert Spirituel a une production sonore, pour un ensemble baroque, qui ne ressemble à aucune des autres orchestres que je connaisse. Nous avons beaucoup de fondamentale, de puissance, de virtuosité, de détail parce que *tout le monde* est important. C'est un travail de tous les jours : il n'y en a pas un qui a le droit de s'asseoir s'il n'est pas efficace à 100 % parce que je le sens, j'en ai besoin. Et par là même, chacun sent qu'il est vraiment important – donc il sera bon. En effet, c'est exigeant : on n'a pas de temps à perdre et on ne perd pas de temps.

C'est comme mener une " maison ". Moi, je suis fasciné par les palaces. Or l'esprit d'un palace, c'est ça : tout est réglé, le client est important, et *tout le monde* est concerné *par tout*. Je revendique Le Concert Spirituel comme une maison où chacun a sa place, et donc où chacun est *responsable*. »

PERSONNALITÉS

« Dans la musique, rien ne se fait sans rencontres. Et il en existe des personnalités formidables ! Que serait Le Concert Spirituel sans le tonitruant René Koering, le passionné Benoît Dratwicki, le cultivé Michel Franck, le détonnant Laurent Brunner, l'inclassable Michèle Paradon, l'exigeant Emmanuel Hondré et tous les infatigables directeurs de festivals à travers la France qui font rayonner leur territoire, du plus petit au plus grand, comme René Martin avec sa Folle Journée ? Sans compter tous ces tenaces qui réussissent à convaincre aux quatre coins du monde de programmer Boismortier, Bouteiller, Le Prince ou Benevolo, de Mexico à Pékin, de Séoul à Varaždin, de Varsovie à Istanbul ! »

RIRE

« Qu'est-ce que j'ai ri avec les danseurs quand j'étais à l'Opéra de Paris ! Mais j'ai ri parce que c'était très dur, pour tout le monde. Le rire est un exutoire formidable, et les danseurs sont vraiment très drôles. Beaucoup de gens me critiquent parce que je désacralise le profil de chef en faisant le clown. Un pilote de 747, je comprends, mais un chef d'orchestre ? Il n'y a pas mort d'homme. Quand je fais le clown, je travaille à fond. Et ensuite, ce n'est pas parce que je fais le clown que je perds mes facultés d'analyse, d'écoute et de décision. Mon exigence reste la même.

Mais attention : si j'ai l'air de m'amuser sur scène, ce n'est qu'une impression. Je suis *mort* de trac ! Et si ça ne se voit pas, c'est que c'est un métier. Je ne vais pas aller communiquer mon stress à tout le monde alors que je suis payé pour gérer le stress de tout le monde !

J'utilise beaucoup le rire en répétition. Les informations musicales et techniques sont ainsi noyées dans l'humour, qui a deux facultés : détendre tout le monde quand on est très concentrés – on ne peut pas être concentrés trois heures d'affilée – et changer le son – quand on est détendus, le centre de gravité part très bas et on a beaucoup de fondamentale. Si on rigole de temps en temps, les musiciens respirent mieux, les oreilles s'ouvrent, et ça avance vite. Que des avantages ! »

VOIX

« Le Concert Spirituel n'aurait pas pu exister sans les voix, sans le chœur. De toute façon, c'est l'idéal esthétique de l'époque baroque, il ne faut pas l'oublier, qui cherche à imiter la nature. Or qu'est-ce que la nature ? C'est la voix. J'aurais été déçu que Le Concert Spirituel ne soit qu'un orchestre.

Par contre, on aurait pu se limiter à la musique religieuse, ça oui, parce que le grand motet, c'est l'opéra français sans les emmerdements de la mise en scène, des décors, des costumes : vous êtes votre propre metteur en scène. Vous faites de l'opéra avec le même discours, le même orchestre, le même chœur, le même nombre de solistes. Le langage est *exactement* le même ! Dans un motet, vous avez tempêtes, tremblements de terre, passions amoureuses, septièmes, neuvièmes – comme dans l'opéra. C'est parfois même mieux parce qu'il faut être plus démonstratif pour suppléer au manque de support visuel.

Ce qui me touche dans une voix ? Tout ! Pour le chœur, je ne cherche pas forcément de jolies voix mais un assemblage de voix qui ne soient surtout pas toutes pareilles. Si vous voulez créer un bon pupitre, il faut tout un éventail de couleurs différentes. Vous décuplerez ainsi votre palette d'expressivité sonore. Donc pour le chœur, je ne cherche surtout pas un modèle unique de voix. C'est ce qui fait que Le Concert Spirituel est reconnaissable – à sa palette sonore, à un certain aplomb. Pour les solistes, cela dépend du rôle et de l'œuvre. J'aime bien être à l'aise avec quelqu'un qui veut travailler, qui ne va pas rester bloqué sur ses positions, sur sa voix, ses aigus, ses graves, sa respiration, sa partition… Qui va accepter de se mettre par exemple en faiblesse si le rôle le demande.»

FAINÉANT

« Moi, je suis un fainéant dans l'âme. C'est peut-être ce qui m'a amené à analyser, pour être efficace et économe de mon énergie. Et puis j'aime beaucoup observer – et j'ai eu des places d'où je pouvais le faire. Ce qui continue à me faire avancer aujourd'hui est un faisceau de choses : d'abord, je n'ai pas été éduqué comme un chef d'orchestre, j'ai appris la direction à l'issue d'études classiques, assez brièvement. Je suis tout de suite entré à l'Opéra de Paris, où j'ai pu analyser les témoignages que je recevais. Je n'ai pas eu un cursus de travail de direction classique.

J'ai eu la chance d'être à l'Opéra de Paris pendant huit ans, occupant à peu près tous les postes – huit ans au bout desquels j'en ai eu assez de ne pas avoir à *prendre de décision musicale* ; je voulais m'occuper un peu plus de moi. En tant que pianiste, j'étais déjà du côté interprète, j'ai donc pu voir ce qu'on *subissait* d'un chef. J'étais aussi chanteur, j'ai pu voir aussi ce qu'on ne *voulait pas subir* d'un chef. J'apprends souvent par la négative : c'est très important de savoir ce qu'on ne veut pas reproduire parce qu'on en a souffert. Ce n'est pas difficile : il faut *analyser* – mais c'est un phénomène qu'on oublie souvent. »

BOISMORTIER

« C'est un génie, vraiment ! Tout simple, pas m'as-tu-vu, pas didactique comme Rameau. Chaque fois que l'on écoute sa musique, c'est dimanche matin, ça sent le croissant, il fait beau et le chien vous fait des câlins. C'est ça, Boismortier. Pendant dix ans, j'ai comparé les thèmes communs à Rameau et à Boismortier, les inventions orchestrales : Boismortier arrive toujours le premier. Il est très peu joué parce que, comme Poulenc, il est dilettante. Tellement génial que ce qu'il écrit est parfait, mais comme il gagne de l'argent, il dérange tout le monde, M. Rameau le premier. Physiologiquement, à jouer, sa musique est absolument formidable : c'est organique – pour tous les instruments pour lesquels il a composé. On fabrique du bonheur à chaque mesure ! La moindre petite sonate pour flûte seule est magnifique. C'est vraiment mon compositeur fétiche. »

MUSIQUE FRANÇAISE

« Il y a une notion d'entité patrimoniale. Ce n'est pas la musique pour la musique : elle est une partie de cette culture française dans laquelle je me sens bien ; je ne la sépare pas de la peinture impressionniste ou de l'histoire de la danse ou de la littérature, que j'adore, de l'architecture, du mobilier, des costumes… Quand je travaillais avec Serge Lifar, j'avais l'impression d'être en lien, en ligne directe avec cette histoire qui partait de Lully.

Le plaisir de jouer cette musique française, de découvrir encore aujourd'hui des partitions reste intact. Je me sens très bien là-dedans : je me sens très bien de l'expliquer, parce que j'ai des clés, et pas seulement des clés musicales. J'ai des éclairages à apporter, qui me servent pour toute la musique que j'aborde, baroque ou pas.

Rien n'existe sans le bâti rhétorique, le symbolisme. J'arrive de cette culture-là en ayant étudié les répertoires anciens, ce qui me permet de tout aborder avec une même grille de lecture. Toutes ces découvertes sur la musique baroque d'il y a quelques décennies ont changé l'interprétation de la musique baroque mais aussi de l'interprétation de toute la musique qui suit. »

LANGUE

« Ce qui me fait vibrer dans la musique française ? La langue tout simplement. C'est ma langue maternelle – c'est un trésor incroyable que de posséder une langue. Et Lully utilise la même que Poulenc, donc le travail est le même : il y a des accents prosodiques, des liaisons, des i et des a et des u. Si vous scandez le texte à plat, vous avez déjà le rythme. Le compositeur y pose ses rythmes à lui. Vous avez ensuite les hauteurs de son avec les inflexions du texte, et c'est réglé !

Je ne fais pas de la musique : je fais du mot. Si on ne comprend pas le mot, on ne comprend pas la poésie ; si on ne comprend pas la poésie, on ne comprend pas l'action, et on ne sait pas pourquoi on est là ! Ça n'intéresse personne, à l'époque de Lully, d'aller écouter quelque chose que l'on ne comprend pas. On va voir *Armide* de M. Quinault, sur une musique de Lully – c'est un texte avant tout. Et Rameau dit qu'il préfère avoir dans ses interprètes une actrice ayant une assez jolie voix plutôt qu'une chanteuse.

L'opéra, c'est ça : la mise en musique d'un texte. On n'a pas besoin en soi de la musique, c'est juste un geste qui accompagne pour *bien dire*. Il faut au départ une voix intelligible, compréhensible, intelligente. On ne fait pas de la musique d'ambiance. Souciez-vous du mot, mettez votre énergie à comprendre le mot. Les auteurs sont tellement savants, ils connaissent tellement la physiologie du chant qu'ils ont architecturé leur musique sur les muscles pour être efficace. Donc faites confiance aux mots. C'est ce que je dis aux solistes, qui font souvent passer leur interprétation en premier au lieu d'observer et d'utiliser leur technique sans passion. Résultat : ils surdosent, et on ne comprend rien. Quand ils se rendent compte qu'avec trois fois moins d'énergie ils sont plus compréhensibles, c'est gagné. C'est une grosse aide physiologique, un outil très simple de persuasion de l'auditoire ; une fois qu'ils ont compris ça, ils s'en servent avec délectation. Il y a un vrai bonheur du son du texte : on sent que tout s'ouvre, on a une portée, une projection, on est connecté, tout est logique. »

PRIX DE ROME
« Qui passait le Prix de Rome pour entrer à la Villa Médicis ? Les élèves du Conservatoire de Paris, donc l'élite des apprentis. Dans cette élite de la classe, les professeurs, qui étaient, eux, de grandes stars, choisissaient leurs meilleurs élèves. Donc, l'élite de l'élite. Et cette élite d'élite allait concourir pour le Prix de Rome, donc c'était l'élite de l'élite de l'élite. Et l'élite de l'élite de l'élite de l'élite allait à la Villa Médicis. Donc forcément, ils étaient *tous* très bons, ils savaient tous composer. L'idée, avec le Palazzetto Bru Zane, d'enregistrer les Prix de Rome – trois cents premiers prix et six cents seconds – promettait quelques années d'enregistrement. On est partis là-dessus. Et puis on est allés chercher la famille de ces compositeurs. Les musiciens n'en revenaient pas : ils jouent de la musique du XIXe siècle, et la famille du compositeur vient les écouter en répétition ! Ils avaient perdu de vue que la musique était faite par des gens réels et non pas par des maisons d'édition. Quand Patrice d'Ollone est venu, qu'il a entendu jouer des pièces de concours de son grand-père que son grand-père n'avait jamais entendues, il a pleuré pendant quatre jours. Ça n'était pas une abstraction, c'était Max, son grand-père ! Ça change tout, et ça a changé le son de l'orchestre. C'est ça qui m'intéresse.

Donc voilà : les Prix de Rome et puis les choses infaisables, que les autres ne veulent pas faire, improbables parce que des épopées indéfendables. Avec Alexandre Dratwicki, on a d'abord voulu ne pas effrayer le public, donc on a choisi des noms un peu connus : Debussy, puis Saint-Saëns, Charpentier, Max d'Ollone – une révélation ! –, Dukas – absolument sublime ! –, Gounod… On a retrouvé les partitions de Dukas par hasard dans un carton au Conservatoire, toutes les œuvres qu'il n'avait pas brûlées lui-même – il a détruit les deux tiers de sa production. Tous les envois de Rome, ses cantates, une merveille ! *Polyeucte* – Dukas avait vingt-deux ou vingt-trois ans, on n'était pas encore en 1900… Hollywood lui a tout piqué ! Un génie ! Voilà comment nous avons choisi. On ne se voyait pas commencer par les Véronge de la Nux ou les Deffès.

Ce sont vraiment de grands chefs-d'œuvre, pour lesquels je me passionne doublement : parce que les autres pensent que ce sont des œuvres d'auteurs mineurs, jeunes et sans expérience. Et parce que j'aime ça.

Avec le Palazzetto Bru Zane, on s'arrête en 1920. Je n'irai pas au-delà de toute façon. Messiaen ou Dutilleux, je les ai connus, et il y a d'autres personnes qui font ça mieux que moi.»

DISQUE

« J'enregistre beaucoup. Je suis dans un domaine – la musique ancienne – où on découvre beaucoup, on lit beaucoup, on produit beaucoup. Il *faut* laisser beaucoup, vraiment. Il faut laisser des traces, sans ça on aura travaillé pour rien. Quand je vois que la génération des vingt/ trente ans d'aujourd'hui ne connaît pas certains « grands », ça confirme mon sentiment qu'il faut laisser quelque chose, sinon tout disparaît. Je laisse des ouvrages dont personne n'a le soupçon et dont personne ne s'occupera si on ne le fait pas avec Le Concert Spirituel.

Quand on s'enferme pour faire un disque, on est coupé du monde et on travaille absolument chaque note. Et on fait, on refait et on re-refait. Ça n'a rien à voir avec le concert. On fait un objet, qui fixe un moment qu'on a dans la tête, sans être impressionné par l'humeur de la journée, les gens qui sont derrière, le courant d'air qui passe en coulisse, etc. Et puis l'énergie n'est pas du tout la même. Vous êtes à fond, il n'y a pas d'abandon. C'est un autre travail que celui du concert, ce qui fait que la qualité d'interprétation est différente. Et puis on se permet des choses en enregistrement qu'on ne se permet pas en concert, et vice versa.

Chaque disque est un souvenir – un souvenir d'efforts physiques – parce que c'est un gros travail, une grosse fatigue, une grosse peine, mais que l'on voudrait voir durer sans fin. C'est le sommet du travail, le travail est abouti. Deux disques m'ont marqué, résolument à l'opposé l'un de l'autre. Le premier est la messe de Striggio à 40 voix : on a eu une équipe ahurissante ! C'était un grand moment, trente ans de recherches. À l'opposé, j'adore aussi celui des sonates pour basse de Boismortier, pour quatre basses d'archet, deux théorbes, nous étions deux au clavier, Boismortier au milieu de tout ça. Uniquement des instruments de basses, le sommet du bonheur ! Et le disque est une merveille. Striggio n'existerait pas si le travail fait avec Boismortier n'avait pas existé. »

SAINT-RIQUIER

« La directrice du centre culturel de Saint-Riquier est venue me chercher sans savoir *du tout* que je tenais les orgues de Saint-Riquier il y a quarante-cinq ans et que j'étais né à huit kilomètres. On s'est rencontrés à Istanbul. Moi je n'avais pas du tout prévu de retourner dans la région. J'avais bien quelques amis mais que je ne voyais plus ou rarement. Et là, j'ai dit "oui". En un coup de téléphone, j'ai trouvé quarante bénévoles, rappelé mes anciens copains que je connaissais depuis l'âge de dix ans. Et j'ai décidé de faire traduire les programmes et les dossiers de presse en picard.

Une demi-heure avant le grand concert, avant de faire rentrer le public, on ferme l'église pour voir si tout est en état. Les gens font la queue, et deux acteurs présentent le programme en picard. La première fois, ça a déconcerté tous les bourgeois venus de Lille ou d'Amiens ; et ça a fait rire les gens du coin, qui n'en revenaient pas. Tout le monde s'est mis à parler avec son voisin ! Ensuite, quand ils ont vu qu'on leur distribuait un programme écrit en français et en picard, quel brouhaha dans la salle ! Ceux qui ne lisaient pas le picard se le faisaient expliquer, et les picardisants étaient si contents ! Il y avait de vrais échanges dans le public. Et les gens aujourd'hui collectionnent ces programmes, ils nous demandent ceux qui leur manque, on réimprime ! »

TRANSMISSION

« J'aime faire des académies et des master classes, où j'ai trente-cinq à quarante étudiants d'une même génération ; on est ensemble pendant quinze jours et on travaille sur un projet du soir au matin. Puis on se sépare… et je les retrouve dans le métier. Réussir à les faire approcher de l'harmonie, sur un temps condensé, est extrêmement formateur. Ils iront à la quête de quelque chose toute leur vie, ça leur donne une direction. Je leur pose beaucoup de questions qu'ils ne se posent pas. À eux de chercher, de faire le cheminement et de trouver la réponse, et surtout de déduire pourquoi ça marche à chaque fois. Il faut qu'ils analysent les choses.»

MUSIC HALL

« C'est à New York, où j'allais souvent avec l'Opéra de Paris, que j'ai découvert la comédie musicale et Broadway. À Londres aussi. J'étais fasciné : c'est une musique qui rend heureux ! Tout le monde doit être très bon, sinon vous êtes remplacé le lendemain. Ça m'amuserait de monter une comédie musicale ; je m'en approche déjà avec *Don Quichotte chez la Duchesse…* De toute façon, c'est nous qui l'avons inventée, la comédie musicale, avec Lully. Il vous faut un bon livret, une bonne histoire, un bon compositeur, et surtout un bon décorateur et un bon chorégraphe : qu'est-ce d'autre qu'une comédie musicale ? Racine et Quinault disaient qu'avec soixante mots ils pouvaient faire une tragédie, et si vous regardez bien, ce sont toujours les mêmes. La tragédie lyrique, c'est ça ! On y va pour la totalité des arts sur scène ! On est plus impressionné par une machine que par la musique de Lully.

Dans le genre, la musique de Michel Legrand m'émeut profondément. C'est quand même le sommet de la musique française. Il a été élève de Nadia Boulanger, il sait écrire une symphonie de Beethoven s'il veut. C'est un génie, immédiatement reconnaissable, comme Ravel, Beethoven ou Debussy. Immédiatement !

Ma mélodie du bonheur, ça reste mes enfants qui se chamaillent. Quand on est ensemble, il arrive toujours un moment où ils se disputent. Je trouve ça formidable. Ils sont autour de moi, je n'existe absolument plus ! Ils sont adultes, ils existent pour eux-mêmes, moi je suis là, je ne les dérange pas, je les regarde, ils sont beaux, puis ils se rabibochent, et ça recommence. C'est ça la mélodie du bonheur : mes enfants. »

Propos recueillis les 16 juin, 29 septembre et 3 octobre 2016 par Claire Boisteau

THE MUSICAL MiLLe Feuille

of HERVÉ NIQUET

Hervé Niquet lets us in on some of the secrets of his personal cuisine with what one might call a 'musical millefeuille', featuring memories, whims, passions, and even the odd rant, specially prepared for the thirtieth anniversary of Le Concert Spirituel. Tuck in!

Conductor of choirs and orchestras, founder of Le Concert Spirituel, great lover of French music (Baroque in particular, but not only), pioneering explorer of Prix de Rome cantatas with the Palazzetto Bru Zane, madcap comedian in the operatic stagings of his friends Shirley et Dino, keen amateur gardener and reader of San-Antonio père, architecture enthusiast, wacky early morning commentator on France Musique, unconditional fan of all things Picard and artistic director of the Saint-Riquier Festival . . . Hervé Niquet doesn't take himself seriously, yet takes everything he does very seriously indeed. He's a funny sort of humanist, or just a sort of funny humanist, who loves his musicians – and whose musicians love him back. A man who doesn't hesitate to get his hands in the mix, whose mouth waters at the idea of cooking up delicious dishes for his friends and who is a respectful admirer of chefs like Bernard Pacaud. Here he lets us in on some of the secrets of his personal cuisine with what one might call a 'musical millefeuille', featuring memories, whims, passions, and even the odd rant, specially prepared for the thirtieth anniversary of Le Concert Spirituel. Tuck in!

NUNS

'I learned a lot from the nuns who taught me in Abbeville: architecture (we lived in a building dating from between the fifteenth and eighteenth centuries), the organ, music . . . Everyone wore the same smock, and I can tell you that wearing a uniform really gets your imagination going! I had my entire schooling there, from nursery school to *baccalauréat*, for a whole series of interdependent reasons.

'Nowadays I don't even think about the sequence of events, but it all happened quite naturally: my first piano teacher, who conducted the parish choir, sent me to another teacher in Amiens; I sang in the choir, I played the organ, then I conducted the choir myself. That's always the way it works in parishes: one thing leads to another. Then you start writing things, after which you take a harmony class, then counterpoint. You realise that it's useful and very simple if you can put your lesson into practice the next day. It's very exciting because it's always grounded in some kind of performance. I wrote plenty of masses and hymns and things like that! That's what learning is all about.'

PIANO

'My mother decided I should have piano lessons, probably because she saw it as some kind of social advancement. My father had brought an instrument home: it arrived in a cattle truck – it came from a farm and he'd bought it for ten francs! As I was getting a bit bored with my teachers, my father got hold of some scores he had bought by the kilo in a pawnshop - all the works they used to have in good bourgeois households. So I started to read my way through all the operettas, all the Beethoven symphonies in piano reduction, for example *La Cocarde de Mimi-Pinson...* who knows that one?! It really made me laugh, and as a result I read all of Mozart, Mendelssohn, Haydn and Wagner that way . . . Since I detested sport, I read music instead…everything I could get my hands on! That's how I got to know the classics, all on my own – and when I arrived at the Paris Opéra at the age of twenty, I was able to sight-read anything at any time of day or night, so I didn't regret it for one moment.'

MAURICE RAVEL

'When I was young I didn't have access to very much. But when I went to take my piano lessons in Amiens, at around fourteen or fifteen, my teacher was Marie-Cécile Morin, who had been a classmate of Samson François under Marguerite Long. When she was about twelve herself and was practising pieces by Ravel, Marguerite would say to her: "Work hard on your pieces, and I'll ask Maurice to come to the next lesson." Maurice *Ravel!* And she would come back with her little score, Éditions Leduc… I can still remember it. She had sat with Ravel by her side, who would correct her, mark the phrasing and fingering, and tell her what she should think about. And when I worked on Ravel with her, she would say to me: "Next week I'll bring my score." Her score *annotated by Ravel*. That was my first contact with original sources.

The red pencil mark, the little note at the foot of the page, the little smile, the little drawing... all in Maurice Ravel's hand! For me, he was somebody who belonged to history, to books, not to real life. That had quite an impact. And later, when I was at the Opéra de Paris, I met Madeleine Milhaud who would tell me about her husband and Satie, Colette or Cocteau, and Serge Lifar, who told me about Bakst, Diaghilev and Picasso. It was as if I was in a history book myself.'

THE TRIGGER

'When I was fifteen, the violinist Pierre Amoyal came to my neck of the woods to give a concert with his wife and a harpsichordist. The latter had a modern instrument from the 1960s, the kind that still worked perfectly despite being thrown from the fourth floor, with five pedals, a hook to tie up the dog, a shelf for pots and pans, all lit up from inside . . . In short, I was fascinated by this instrument that I didn't understand, that I'd never seen before. I was *flabbergasted*! That was the first time I heard Bach or Rameau played on a harpsichord. I went home and asked my grandmother (I'd done my homework on the cost) to lend me some money: "Grandma, I'd like to buy a harpsichord kit. I'd like to have an instrument like that." I abandoned Beethoven, Brahms, Chopin and so on, and immersed myself in all the scores I had – modern, of course – of Rameau and co., to try to understand them. I went to Paris to see the harpsichord maker Marc Ducornet; I bought a little kit from him that I began to build with a friend of mine. I built five, six, seven harpsichords, which I sold afterwards. I wanted to try to understand how it worked. That concert was the trigger. I made the connection with sacred music, which I had played as an organist in the parish choir, and I started to investigate some recordings.

'These days it feels funny to play the harpsichord again. I did it recently in Bruges when I replaced the continuo player in *Don Quichotte chez la Duchesse*. It was as if I'd gone back forty years! I found it funny and so did the musicians. But I don't do it any more. There are people who do it a thousand times better than me.'

DANCE

'I originally came to Paris because I wanted to be a dancer. I had some skill: I could jump, I could turn, I was supple. I'd started in Abbeville, continued at the Amiens Conservatoire, I did three months at the Paris Conservatoire, and then: stop. The idea of having to give up your job at forty because you're getting old really got me down. And then, when you're a dancer, you're a dancer 24/7. You have to look after your body and your flexibility all the time, your whole life. I loved reading, improving my mind, finding things out, and something I'd come across with my piano teacher – those manuscripts – was beginning to play on my mind. So I gave up dancing, and dancing was all the better for it! To pay for my lessons, I used to accompany other dance classes. Noëlla Pontois, who was a principal dancer at the Opéra de Paris forty years ago, had spotted me in a class and asked me to step in to replace a few accompanists. One thing led to another, and after passing a competitive audition I joined the Opéra as a ballet pianist. After that I also did some chorus and stage accompanying; I carved out a place for myself in the company.

'I learned what it is to have standards at the Opéra de Paris. I went straight from my studies, to working professionally with the best choreographers and dancers in the world. With Nureyev as my boss! There was no period of adjustment or transition, just this terrifying learning process at top speed. It definitely forged my character. I look back on it as an *extremely* intense moment in my life.

'Today, dance helps me not to be cramped in my conducting style. I'm fairly agile, I have long arms and I'm not afraid to open them. Yes I move, yes I walk, but then a lot of things in music are related to dance. I find plenty of musical solutions thanks to dance. And as for accompanying, it's been vital.'

NATIONAL LIBRARY
OF FRANCE

'This was the 1970s, right when the Early Music Revival was getting off the ground, with Christopher Hogwood, Gustav Leonhardt, Jean-Claude Malgoire, René Jacobs and Philippe Herreweghe. I used to go to the open classes given by William Christie in the little rooms at the Conservatoire. It was very intimate: in a corridor, at the back of a dance studio or on a mezzanine. We would set up a harpsichord, and stand around and read through cantatas and other bits and pieces. It was only later that William Christie got his own class. He was indispensable – he was such a fount of knowledge, so sure of himself; he had read *everything*!

'Obviously, I was fascinated, not only because he had an answer to everything but also because, unlike the orchestral conductors I saw at the Opéra, he talked about rhetoric, madrigalism, history, musicology, organology, scholarly research, autograph manuscripts! I had just arrived from my small town, where the only collection of music belonged to the parish priest and the nuns at school; whereas in Paris, for seven francs, I could get a reader's pass for the Bibliothèque Nationale de France and get access to the manuscripts of Campra and so many others! I still remember how the chair felt in the reading room on the fifth floor… the first time I went there, I couldn't get over it! I was twenty years old and I went there every week, for whole days at a time. I was totally hooked!

'The two people I went to hear, William Christie and Nikolaus Harnoncourt, had answers because they hadn't *learned* but *looked*. At that time they were among the only ones who knew what they knew because they had looked for the answer themselves. And when they didn't have time to look, they sent us to look for them. That's what gave me a taste for this perpetual treasure hunt.'

FANATICS

'Forty years ago, early repertories were ripe for rediscovery. Everything remained to be done. Today we still have musicologists who are fanatical about primary research, consumed by passion, who bring us solutions we didn't have thirty, twenty or even ten years ago. And there are young ensembles who go looking for repertoire, who adopt a different approach – because we're more and more at ease in this music now. How refreshing!

'We have to admit that we're lucky to have as artistic director of the Centre de Musique Baroque de Versailles a total madman and fount of knowledge in the form of Benoît Dratwicki. If it weren't for him, whole sections of French repertoire would still be lying neglected.

'Thirty years after the creation of Le Concert Spirituel, I continue to take the risk of programming unknown works. I used to run off in all directions at once because I had an appetite for everything. But then, with advancing age, I find I have to channel my energy; now I go more and more for what corresponds to my tastes. If I do Benevolo, it's because I have a penchant for unknown Italian polyphony; if I do a lot of nineteenth and twentieth century music, it's a throwback to my time at the Opéra de Paris. With the Palazzetto Bru Zane and the Centre de Musique Baroque de Versailles, I have alongside me two very solid institutions full of researchers who bring me repertoire that suits my tastes because they know me.'

SUITCASES

'My job is to understand the work, to have a vision of it and to have at my disposal a team of specialist workers – the musicians – who can realise ideas. I have to arrive at rehearsals with my suitcases full of things to pass on – whether it's with Le Concert Spirituel, the Brussels Philharmonic, in Lisbon or in Budapest. Each project is *really* important and deserves all the work we invest in it. Musicians haven't put in fifteen years of personal study, spent their youth not going to sport lessons, done hours and hours of scales, sat auditions, in order to be bored out of their minds once they've made it into the profession! They're going to find it pretty tedious if the conductor isn't up to the mark – culturally, socially, in human or even musical terms. As soon as you open the toolbox to talk musicology, understanding, rhetoric, everybody's happy! As soon as someone *contributes* something, even something contradictory, unexpected, the fruit of research, of intelligence, the debate is open, and that's bound to give the musicians' life a new perspective. When I say "life", it really is their life, because musicians spend six or even ten hours a day with their instrument, with music. A conductor cannot underestimate the commitment, the work, the energy that demands. An orchestra isn't a tool: it's people.'

CAREER

'It's not pride that I feel about my career. It's more happiness than pride. Even now, when I go to the rue de

Madrid, to what was the Paris Conservatoire when I was twenty – a place where I was *never* accepted despite all the entrance exams I took – I feel pain. When I was at the Opéra de Paris, relations between the musicians and répétiteurs at the Opéra, and professors at the Conservatoire were very close. So I was often asked to write tests for Conservatoire students, entry papers, sight-reading tests, variations, even though they hadn't wanted me there! The complex I felt as a result spurs me on not to *prove* but to *seek*. I'm never convinced I know enough, and that's what constantly pushes me to get back to work.'

TROUPE

'At the Paris Opéra, I learned how to live in a company, to be part of a troupe, so when I enter an opera house now I very quickly get to know everybody – the production manager, the props manager, the wardrobe supervisor, the chief dresser, the machinist, the lighting person - and all of them by their first names . . . It's so much faster, more efficient, healthier and simpler to address people by their first names. There are all these people backstage who spend their lives in the theatre, who are never given the credit they deserve, who are always in the dark – whereas they are artists who make it possible for us to appear in the limelight. *Each person* is important. *Each place* is important. And that brings harmony, and where there's harmony, there's the correct tuning, rhythm, everything you need to bring out what's written in a score. If there is harmony, there is everything – but to achieve that, everyone must be in their place and regard that place as essential.'

BRAZZAVILLE

'If someone is not connected with reality, if an artist isn't in touch with real life, he's a jerk! I've been in Africa a lot, especially in the Congo – under the Mobutu regime: I became friendly with what was left of a conservatoire in Brazzaville. With a singer and a guitarist – and me on keyboard – we went to meet teachers there for a fortnight; we worked with them, we played with them. They didn't have a pencil, not a scrap of paper. For years, via the embassy, I sent them kilos of paper, kilos of pencils. Then one day the parcel came back: there was no conservatoire left: they had all been killed. Those people had been killed because they were trying to learn an art that didn't fit in with the ideas of the ruling dictatorship. So you can be sure that now I can't stand having a musician in front of me who isn't concentrating 100% in rehearsal or in concert. I can still see the faces of all those friends who died because of music . . .'

DIRECTORS

'I've had some very good experiences with directors, notably with Christoph Marthaler, Romeo Castellucci, and of course Shirley and Dino. Those four are extremely cultured people, who work very hard. They have different ways of functioning but they all love their job. Take Christoph Marthaler: everything is ready in his head, but he doesn't know what he's going to do. We live together for five weeks, we rehearse the opera together, we don't know where we're going, but it all works out on the night. Romeo is an extraordinary illustrator and creator of images: he leads you into his storybook. It's like *Alice in Wonderland* - you can't believe your eyes. And Gilles and Corinne[1] know Racine, Corneille and Molière like the back of their hands, they know how to handle a troupe, and everything is ready the moment you arrive to work. I also greatly enjoyed working with Mariame Clément. She's someone who is terrifically well-prepared, very open, who can make poetry out of the smallest change of scene, and who respects even the most junior person.

'Nothing is ever simple, and when there are difficulties, you have to cope with them. If I've agreed to do a production, I have to see it through to the end – and then I have to protect the people I've hired. Sometimes you have experiences that are not so great, but you still manage to make something out of them. And then conducting an operatic production means dealing with a host of worries of all kinds. You have to be ready to save every situation, so as not to endanger the artists on stage.'

SHIRLEY & DINO

'I discovered a sense of theatre with Corinne and Gilles Benizio – really only quite recently – but above all I discovered that it's an extremely hard profession. It takes so much work! But once you get there, it's great. I used to take myself very seriously when I was doing tragedy, but when I saw how difficult it is to do comedy . . . ! In a tragedy, the guidelines are very clear. In comedy, you have to keep your wits about you, and above all you have to be a mathematician in order to react in a heartbeat. Being just about right won't do: you have to have a superior sense of rhythm, to be demanding with others and with yourself.

'Gilles and Corinne and I share the same tastes for the same things because we belong to the same generation. We were there for the early days of television; we loved watching *La Piste aux* étoiles, Les Branquignols[2] and so on. We laugh at the same things and we like a job well done. Like me, they weren't born with a silver spoon in their mouths, and it has been a slog for them to get to where they are today. We've always been able to make do on a shoestring, and it doesn't scare us. Coco loves cooking, so do I. Gilles loves eating. I'm useless with wine; he knows all about it. He loves motorbikes; I hate them. We've become great friends, and our kids too. But it all started because we had great affinities in our work.'

1 The real names of the husband-and-wife directing team known professionally as 'Shirley et Dino'. (Translator's note)
2 Respectively, a circus show that ran on French television from 1964 to 1978 and a troupe of actors and singers, active in the theatre and the cinema from the 1940s to the 1970s, which nurtured many of the best-known comedians of that period. (Translator's note)

LE CONCERT SPIRITUEL

'Starting your own business, as I did with Le Concert Spirituel – having to use your own resources, where every penny counts, having to go out and hire people yourself, promote concerts, put together a programme, write out scores by hand because you don't have any other means (I did the orchestral parts for our first thirty discs, a colossal task) – is character-building. I know how much all of that costs. To put together a team of friends that works well for thirty years is quite something!

'These days it has become a wonderful community that can work harmoniously of its own accord. That's the result of an education lasting thirty years. In the old days, to produce a sound I liked with the Le Concert Spirituel, I needed a whole rehearsal session; now it takes me ten minutes. When new musicians arrive, their older colleagues take them in hand very quickly to insert them into the fabric of our sound. I find that very nice. And unlike some ensembles who put the new kids on the back desks or in posts where they aren't exposed to danger, we put them in the front line, sitting beside the leader. They're not there to make up the numbers! It's rather gratifying for them, and we're almost always rewarded for the risk we take – it's really heartening.'

GUARDIAN ANGELS

'Those who believed in me and my craziest projects, come hell or high water! Without them, I wouldn't be here today . . . Jean and Nicole Bru, of course, the most important meeting of my life! With Le Concert Sprituel and the Fondation Bru, which created the Palazzetto Bru Zane - Centre de Musique Romantique Française in Venice, Nicole Bru has saved more than three centuries of French music. That deserves more than a medal – I don't know, maybe a place reserved for her in the Panthéon? Martine Tridde and the Fondation BNP Paribas were also great partners, first in Canada then with Le Concert Spirituel, for several years! Now I have the enormous good fortune of being supported by Mécénat Musical Société Générale, the principal patron of Le Concert Spirituel, and by Groupe SMA. Not surprisingly, those who manage the cultural programmes in these companies are cultured, music-loving, inquisitive, visionary people, and some of them are discreet and enthusiastic amateur musicians. The Ministry of Culture and Paris City Council are also faithful supporters of our musical adventure.'

MONEY

'When you work in the music world, you always have to look for money. There are two things that go together, the two reasons I'm in this profession: (a) to eat, and (b) to meet people. Taking only Le Concert Spirituel into account, I provide work for between 200 and 250 people every year – the figure varies from one year to another. If I calculate on average one family per employee, that makes a thousand people. If I shut up shop, that means hard times for those people. If you don't think about the money coming in and the money going out, you don't exist anymore. A euro really is a euro. Every time I get on the podium, a sum of money is spent. So I can't get it wrong: I have to read the scores and be sure of what I'm doing. We're not going to put something on if we run the risk of sinking without trace.

'The artist in an ivory tower is a myth. Or else the artist in question is fabulously rich – that does happen, but you can see what the result is. No, I have a pastoral duty. Everybody has to be good, everybody has to be alert, otherwise the music won't be any good. To get back to (b), music is just an excuse to meet people. I'm aware that the time when everyone has the most fun, the musicians and myself, is during rehearsals. To give a good concert, to succeed in communicating everything that has been amassed during rehearsals, is the icing on the cake.'

LUXURY HOTEL

'There is no such thing as a concert with a conductor but without musicians. It simply doesn't exist! I have to ensure that each instrumentalist or singer takes up his or her rightful place. Because it's in that exchange that things happen. Le Concert Spirituel has a particular sound for a Baroque ensemble that is unlike any other orchestra that I know. We have a really a lot of fundamental harmonics, power, virtuosity and attention to detail, because *everybody* is important. I have to work at that every day: nobody has the right to sit in the ensemble if they're not 100% efficient, because I can sense that, and I need that 100% efficiency. But because of that, everyone feels that they're really important – so they'll be good. It's a demanding process: we don't have any time to waste, and we don't waste any time. 'It's like running a "big house". Personally, I'm fascinated by luxury hotels. And the spirit of a luxury hotel is exactly that: everything is organised, the clientele is important, and *everyone* is concerned about *everything*. I like to claim that Le Concert Spirituel is like a big house in which everyone has his or her own place, and therefore everyone is *responsible*.'

PERSONALITIES

'In the music world, nothing can be done without meeting other people. And there are some wonderful personalities! What would Le Concert Spirituel be without the thunderous René Koering, the passionate Benoît Dratwicki, the cultured Michel Franck, the quirky Laurent Brunner, the indefinable Michèle Paradon, the rigorous Emmanuel Hondré, and all the indefatigable directors of festivals all over France who cover their own territory, large or small, like René Martin with his Folle Journée? Not to mention all those persistent administrators who manage to convince concert promoters at the four corners of the globe to put on Boismortier, Bouteiller, Le Prince or Benevolo, from Mexico to Beijing, from Seoul to Varaždin, from Warsaw to Istanbul!'

LAUGHTER

'How I used to laugh with the dancers when I was at the Opéra de Paris! But I would laugh because it was very tough, for everybody. Laughter is a great way of relieving tension, and dancers are very funny people. Many people criticise me because I knock the image of the conductor off its pedestal by clowning around. I can understand that reaction if I were an airline pilot, but a conductor? It's not a life-or-death issue. When I fool around, I'm still working at full throttle. And the fact that I'm playing the clown doesn't mean I lose my ability to analyse, listen and make decisions. My rigour remains the same.

'But take note: if I look as if I'm having fun on stage, it's just an impression. I'm *dying* of stage fright! And if no one can see that, it's because I've got a job to do. I'm not going to pass on my stress to everyone else when I'm paid to manage their stress!

'I use laughter a great deal in rehearsal. That way, the musical and technical information is watered down by the humour, which has two benefits: making everyone relax when they're concentrating hard – you can't stay concentrated for three hours at a stretch – and changing the sound: when people are relaxed, the centre of gravity starts very low and you get a bigger proportion of fundamental harmonics. If they have a laugh from time to time, the musicians breathe better, their ears open, and we progress faster. There are only advantages!'

VOICES

'Le Concert Spirituel couldn't have existed without voices, without the choir. In any case, we mustn't forget that the voice was the aesthetic ideal of the Baroque era, which sought to imitate nature. And what is nature? The voice. I would have been disappointed if Le Concert Spirituel had only been an instrumental ensemble.

'On the other hand, we could quite plausibly have restricted ourselves to sacred music, because the *grand motet* is just French opera without the hassle of the production, the sets, the costumes: you are your own director. You're performing opera with the same discourse, the same orchestra, the same chorus, the same number of soloists. The language is *exactly* the same! In a motet, you've got storms, earthquakes, amorous passions, seventh and ninth chords – just as in an opera. Sometimes it's even better, because you have to be more demonstrative to compensate for the lack of a visual dimension.

'What is it that touches me in a voice? Everything! For the choir, I don't necessarily look for beautiful voices, but for an assemblage of voices that, above all, must not be all the same. If you want to create a good soprano or bass section, you need a whole range of different timbres. That way you make your expressive sound palette much broader. So, for the choir, I don't look for a single model of a voice. That's what makes Le Concert Spirituel recognisable – for its sound palette, for a certain aplomb.

'When it comes to the soloists, it depends on the role and the music we're performing. I like to be comfortable with flexible people who want to work, who don't take a rigid attitude with their voice, their high notes, their low notes, their breathing, with the score etc.. . . With people who, for example, agree to put themselves in a position of weakness if the role demands it.'

LAZINESS

'I'm a lazy person at heart. Perhaps that's what prompted me to analyse things, to be efficient and use my energy sparingly. And also I like to observe a lot – and I've had jobs where I could do that. What still makes me tick today is a nexus of things. First of all, I wasn't trained as a conductor; I learned conducting at the end of a standard course of musical studies, and fairly briefly. Then I went straight to the Opéra de Paris, where I was able to analyse the feedback I got. I didn't follow a standard course of training in conducting.

'I was fortunate to be at the Opéra de Paris for eight years, occupying just about every post – eight years at the end of which I was fed up with not being able to *take a musical decision*; I wanted to pay more attention to myself. As a pianist, I was already on the performer's side of the divide, so I could see what people had to *suffer* from a conductor. I was also a singer, and so I could see what people *didn't want to suffer* from a conductor. I often learn from negative experiences: it's very important to know what you don't want to reproduce because you've suffered from it. That's not hard to do: you have to *analyse* – but it's an approach that is often forgotten.'

BOISMORTIER

'He really is a genius! Quite simple, not a show-off, not didactic like Rameau. Every time you listen to his music, it's like Sunday morning, you can smell the croissants, it's sunny outside and the dog is snuggling up to you. That's Boismortier. For ten years I compared the themes and orchestral inventions common to Rameau and Boismortier: Boismortier always came out on top. He's very rarely performed because, like Poulenc, he was an amateur. He was such a genius that everything he wrote is perfect, but because he earned money with it, he got everyone's back up, starting with Monsieur Rameau. Physiologically, his music is absolutely wonderful to play: it's organic for all the instruments he wrote for. You're producing happiness in every bar! The smallest flute sonata is magnificent. He really is my favourite composer.'

FRENCH MUSIC

'There's the idea that it's a patrimonial entity. It's not just music for music's sake: it's a part of French culture in which I feel at home. I don't separate it from Impressionist painting or the history of dance or literature, which I adore, or architecture, furniture, couture . . . When I worked with Serge Lifar, I had the impression I was in a direct lineage from that point in history beginning with Lully. The pleasure of performing French music, of discovering new works, has remained with me even today. I feel very comfortable with it: I feel comfortable explaining it, because I have the keys to it, and not only musical keys. I feel I have a perspective on it which serves me for all the music I tackle, Baroque or not. 'Nothing exists without the rhetorical framework, the symbolism. I come from that culture, having studied early repertoire, which enables me to approach everything with a single interpretative template. All those discoveries about Baroque music from a few decades ago have changed the interpretation of Baroque repertoire, but also of all the music that comes after it.'

LANGUAGE

'What is it that thrills me about French music? Quite simply, the language. It's my mother tongue – it's an incredible treasure to possess a language. And Lully uses the same language as Poulenc, so the work is the same: there are prosodic accents, liaisons, "i" and "a" and "u" vowels. If you read the text aloud in singsong fashion, you already have the rhythm. The composer adds his own rhythm to that. Then you have the pitches and the inflections of the text, and that's it sorted!'

'I don't do music; I do words. If you don't understand the word, you don't understand the poetry; if you don't understand the poetry, you don't understand the meaning, and then you don't know why you're there! In Lully's day, no one was interested in going to hear something they couldn't understand. When they went to see "*Armide* de M. Quinault, sur une musique de Lully", it was the text that counted above all. And Rameau says he'd prefer an actress with a fairly pretty voice over a singer.

'That's what opera is: the musical setting of a text. You don't need the music in itself, it's just something that exists to help communicate the text. The starting point must be a voice that is intelligible, comprehensible, intelligent. We're not doing background music here. Look after the words, use your energy to understand the words. The authors were so skilled, they were so familiar with the physiology of singing, that they built their music around the vocal muscles in order to communicate effectively. So trust the words. That's what I say to soloists, who often put their performance first instead of observing and using their technique without passion. The result is that they overdose on the voice, and we don't understand anything. When they realise that they're easier to understand when they use a third of their energy, you're home and dry. It's a big physiological aid, a very simple tool for persuading the audience; once they've understood that, they're delighted to use it. There is genuine pleasure in the sound of the text: you feel that everything opens up, the voice carries, it's projected; everything is connected, everything is logical.'

PRIX DE ROME

'Who entered the Prix de Rome competition to get to the Villa Medici? The students of the Paris Conservatoire, that's to say, the élite of those who were learning the trade. Within that élite of the class, the professors, who were themselves great stars, chose their best pupils. So, the élite of the élite. And that élite of the élite went on to compete for the Prix de Rome, so it was the élite of the élite of the élite. And the élite of the élite of the élite of the élite would actually make it to the Villa Medici! So, inevitably, they were *all* very good, they all knew how to compose. The idea, hatched with the Palazzetto Bru Zane, of recording the Prix de Rome winners – three hundred first prizes and six hundred second prizes – looked set to take up several years of recording sessions. So we embarked on the project. And then we went to look for the families of these composers. The musicians couldn't believe their eyes: they're playing music of the nineteenth century, and the composer's family comes to listen to the rehearsals! They had forgotten that music was produced by real people and not by publishing houses. When Patrice d'Ollone came, he heard us playing test pieces by his grandfather that even his grandfather had never heard, and he wept for four days. It wasn't an abstraction, it was Max, his Granddad! That changes everything, and it changed the sound of the orchestra. That's what interests me.

'So there we are: the Prix de Rome winners and then the impractical things, the things nobody else wants to do, the things that are improbable because they're epic and no one can defend them nowadays. To start with, Alexandre Dratwicki and I didn't want to frighten the public away, so we chose names that were known at least to some extent: Debussy, then Saint-Saëns, Gustave Charpentier, Max d'Ollone (a revelation!), Dukas (absolutely sublime!), Gounod . . . We found the Dukas scores by accident in a cardboard box at the Conservatoire, all the works he hadn't burned himself – he destroyed two-thirds of his output. All the compositions he sent back from Rome, his cantatas, with one wonderful piece, *Polyeucte*. Dukas was only twenty-two or twenty-three then, as this was before 1900. Hollywood pinched the lot from him! A genius! That's how we made our selection. We didn't see ourselves starting with names like Véronge de la Nux or Deffès.

'They are truly great masterpieces, which I'm so enthusiastic about for two reasons: first of all, because other people think they're works by minor figures, young and inexperienced; and second, because I love them.

'With the Palazzetto Bru Zane, we stop in 1930. I won't go any further anyway. Messiaen, Dutilleux, I knew them personally, and there are other people who do their music better than I can.'

DISCS

'I record a lot. I work in a field – early music– where we discover a lot, we read a lot, we produce a lot. We *must* leave behind a legacy, we really must. Otherwise we'll have worked for nothing. When I see young 20 and 30 somethings today who don't know certain "great" figures, it confirms my feeling that we must leave our mark, otherwise everything will disappear. I leave behind me works that no one had an inkling of and that no one will take care of if we don't record them with Le Concert Spirituel.

'When you shut yourself away to make a recording, you're cut off from the outside world and you work on absolutely every single note. And you do it, you redo it, and you redo it again. It has nothing to do with concert performance. You're creating an object, fixing a moment you have in your mind, without letting yourself be affected by your mood, the people behind you, the draught coming from backstage, and so on. And the energy isn't at all the same. You're completely concentrated, you never let yourself go. It's a different job from the one you do in concert, which means the quality of the interpretation is different. And you allow yourself to do things on a recording that you wouldn't do in a concert, and vice versa.

'Each disc is a memory – a memory of physical efforts – because it's a huge amount of work, hugely tiring, all blood sweat and tears, because it's something you want to see last forever. It's the summit of your work. Two discs made a particular impact on me, and they couldn't be more different. The first is the Mass for forty voices by Striggio: we had an amazing team! That was a great moment, the climax of thirty years of research. I also loved Boismortier's sonatas for basses, played on four string bass instruments with two theorbos, two of us at the keyboard, and Boismortier in the midst of all that. Only bass instruments, the height of happiness! And the disc is a marvel. Striggio would not exist if the work we did on Boismortier hadn't existed.'

SAINT-RIQUIER

'The director of the cultural centre of Saint-Riquier asked me to come there without having the *slightest idea* that I had played the organ in Saint-Riquier forty-five years ago and that I was born eight kilometres away. We met in Istanbul. I had no intention of going back to the region. I did have a few friends there, but I saw them very rarely if at all. But then I said yes. With a few telephone calls, I found forty volunteer helpers and spoke to my old schoolmates whom I'd known since the age of ten. And I decided to have the programmes and press kits translated into Picard.

'Half an hour before the big concert, before the audience came in, we closed the church to check that everything was in order. People were queuing up outside, and two actors presented the programme in Picard. The first time we did it, all the bourgeois who had come from Lille and Amiens found it unsettling, while it made all the locals laugh – they couldn't believe their ears! Everyone started talking to each other. After that, when they saw they were being handed a programme written in both French and Picard, it caused such a commotion! Those who couldn't read Picard had to have it explained to them, and the Picard-speakers were so happy! There was a genuine exchange in the audience. And now people collect those programmes: they even ask us for the ones they don't have, and we reprint them!'

GIVING BACK

'I like doing academies and masterclasses, where I have between thirty-five and forty students of about the same age; we're together for a fortnight and we work on a project from morning to night. Then we go our separate ways. . . and I come across them again later in the business. It's an extremely formative experience if you can succeed in getting them to tackle harmony in a condensed period of time. It gives them direction, as they then continue to have an inquisitive attitude throughout the rest of their lives. I ask them loads of questions they don't ask themselves. It's up to them to search, to follow the process through and find the answer, and above all to deduce why it works each time. They have to analyse things.

MUSICALS

'I discovered musical comedy and Broadway in New York, where I often went with the Opéra de Paris. I saw musicals in London too. I was fascinated: it's music that makes you happy! Everyone in the cast must be very good, otherwise they replace you the following day. I would enjoy putting on a musical some day; I've already got quite near to it with *Don Quichotte chez la Duchesse*. In any case, the French invented musical comedy, with Lully. You need a good libretto, a good story, a good composer, and above all a good designer and a good choreographer: after all what else is musical comedy? Racine and Quinault said they could produce a tragedy with sixty words; and if you look carefully, it's always the same words. That's what *tragédie lyrique* is! All the arts on stage together! And the audiences were more impressed by a machine than by Lully's music.

'In its way, I find the music of Michel Legrand deeply moving. After all, he really is the peak of French music. A pupil of Nadia Boulanger, he could write a Beethoven symphony if he wanted to. He's a genius, immediately recognisable, just like Ravel, Beethoven or Debussy. Immediately!

'My own personal favourite sound is that of my children squabbling. When we're together, there always comes a point when they start quarrelling. I think that's terrific. They're around me, but I no longer exist! They're adults, they exist for themselves; I'm there, but I don't disturb them. I look at them, they're lovely; then they patch things up, and we start all over again. That's the Sound of Music: my children.'

Edited from interviews with Claire Boisteau on 16 June, 29 September and 3 October 2016

EIN Tutti Frutti

von HERVÉ NIQUET

Hervé Niquet öffnet uns seine Vorratskammer für dieses Tuttifrutti aus Erinnerungen, Launen, Protestschreien und Leidenschaften, das er speziell für das dreißigjährige Bestehen des Concert Spirituel zubereitet hat.

Chorleiter, Dirigent, Gründer des Concert Spirituel, Liebhaber der französischen Musik im allgemeinen und der Barockmusik im besonderen, Erforscher der Werke des Prix du Rome mit dem Palazzetto Bru Zane, verrückter Schauspieler in den Operninszenierungen seiner Freunde Shirley und Dino, Hobbygärtner und Leser von San-Antonio-Krimis, begeisterter Architekturfan, abgefahrener, morgendlicher Feuilletonist bei France Musique, hundertprozentiger Picarde sowie künstlerischer Leiter des Festivals von Saint-Riquier ... Hervé Niquet nimmt sich nicht ernst und macht dennoch mit großem Ernst, was er zu machen hat. Er ist ein komischer Humanist in allen Bedeutungen des Wortes „komisch", er liebt seine Musiker und umgekehrt. Er zögert nicht, selbst Hand anzulegen, und wenn er daran denkt, etwas Köstliches für seine Freunde zu kochen, läuft ihm das Wasser im Mund zusammen. Er hegt eine respektvolle Bewunderung gegenüber Haubenchefs wie Bernard Pacaud und öffnet uns seine Vorratskammer für dieses Tuttifrutti aus Erinnerungen, Launen, Protestschreien und Leidenschaften, das er speziell für das dreißigjährige Bestehen des Concert Spirituel zubereitet hat.

ORDENSSCHWESTERN

„Ich habe bei den Ordensschwestern, von denen ich in Abbeville erzogen wurde, viel gelernt: die Architektur – wir lebten in einem Gebäude aus dem 15. bis 18. Jh. –, die Orgel, die Musik usw. Alle hatten den gleichen Kittel an, und ich kann Ihnen sagen, dass es die Fantasie anregt, eine Uniform zu tragen! Ich habe meine ganze Schulzeit vom Kindergarten bis zum Abitur dort verbracht, u.zw. aus vielen Gründen, die sich ergänzten.

Ich denke nicht einmal mehr nach, wie sich die Geschehnisse aneinanderreihten, jedenfalls war es ganz natürlich: Ich bekam eine andere Klavierlehrerin, die den Kirchenchor leitete und mich nach Amiens schickte; ich sang im Chor, spielte Orgel und dirigierte schließlich den Chor. In den Pfarrgemeinden ist es immer so: Eines bringt das andere mit sich. Und dann versucht man sich zum ersten Mal im Komponieren, also nimmt man Unterricht in Harmonielehre und danach im Kontrapunkt. Man merkt, dass das nützlich und sehr einfach ist, wenn man es gleich am nächsten Tag anwenden kann. Auch ist es anregend, weil es immer mit einer szenischen, theatralischen Realität verknüpft ist. Ich habe Unmengen an Messen, Kirchenliedern und solchen Dingen geschrieben! Wie es eben in der Lehrzeit ist."

KLAVIER

„Meine Mutter hatte beschlossen, mich Klavier lernen zulassen, zweifellos mit dem Hintergedanken eines sozialen Aufstiegs. Mein Vater hatte in einem Viehtransporter ein Instrument nach Hause gebracht, das aus einem Bauernhof kam und ihn 10 Francs gekostet hatte. Da mir mit meinen Lehrern etwas langweilig war, kaufte mir mein Vater bei einem Altwarenhändler kiloweise Noten von all den Werken, die in gut bürgerlichen Häusern zu finden waren. Also las ich mit zwei Fingern alle Operetten, alle Symphonien von Beethoven in Klavierauszügen – *La Cocarde de Mimi-Pinson,* wer kennt das schon? Ich fand das witzig und entzifferte so den ganzen Mozart, Mendelssohn, Haydn, Wagner usw. Da ich Sport hasste, spielte ich alles vom Blatt, was mir unter die Finger kam! So habe ich mir meine Musikliteratur zusammengestellt, ganz allein – und das habe ich nicht bereut: Als ich mit zwanzig Jahren an die Pariser Oper kam, konnte ich zu jeder Zeit jedes beliebige Werk vom Blatt spielen."

MAURICE RAVEL

„Als ich jung war, hatte ich nicht zu Vielem Zugang. Mit vierzehn oder fünfzehn Jahren kam ich nach Amiens, um Klavier zu lernen. Meine Klavierlehrerin war Marie-Cécile Morin, eine Klassenkameradin von Samson François bei Marguerite Long. Als sie selbst zwölf Jahre alt war und Stücke von Ravel erarbeitete, sagte ihr Marguerite Long: „Übe diese Stücke gut, in der nächsten Unterrichtsstunde bitte ich Maurice vorbeizuschauen." Maurice *Ravel!* Und sie kam mit ihren Noten zurück, Édition Leduc, daran erinnere ich mich noch, und sie spielte, während Ravel neben ihr saß und sie korrigierte, Phrasierungen und Fingersätze notierte und ihr sagte, worauf sie ihre Aufmerksamkeit lenken soll. Und als ich mit ihr Ravel erarbeitete, sagte sie zu mir: „Nächste Woche bringe ich meine Noten mit." Ihre *von Ravel mit Anmerkungen versehenen* Noten. Für mich war das der erste Kontakt mit Originalquellen. Der feine rote Bleistiftstrich, das Lächeln, die kleine Zeichnung stammten aus Maurice Ravels Hand! Für mich gehörten sie der Geschichte an, Büchern, aber nicht der Wirklichkeit. Das war ein Schock. Als ich später an der Pariser Oper arbeitete und Madeleine Milhaud kennenlernte, die mir von ihrem Mann, von Satie, Colette oder Cocteau erzählte, während Serge Lifar von Bakst, Djagilew oder Picasso sprach, fühlte ich mich wie in einem Geschichtsbuch."

AUSLÖSER

„Als ich fünfzehn Jahre alt war, kam der Geiger Pierre Amoyal in meine Gegend und gab mit seiner Frau und einer Cembalistin ein Konzert. Letztere hatte ein modernes Instrument aus den 1960er Jahren, das selbst wenn man es aus dem vierten Stockwerk wirft noch tadellos funktioniert mit seinen fünf Pedalen, einem Haken für den Hund, einem Regal für die Töpfe und einer Innenbeleuchtung ... Kurz ich war von diesem Instrument, das ich nicht verstand, das ich noch nie gesehen hatte, fasziniert. *Es hat mich umgehauen!* Damals hörte ich zum ersten Mal Bach oder Rameau auf einem Cembalo. Als ich nach Hause kam, hatte ich mich informiert und bat meine Großmutter, mir Geld zu borgen: „Omi, ich möchte mir einen Fertigbausatz für ein Cembalo kaufen. Ich möchte so ein Instrument haben." Ich ließ Beethoven, Brahms, Chopin links liegen und stürzte mich Hals über Kopf in alle – selbstverständlich modernen – Noten, die ich von Rameau und seinesgleichen besaß, um zu versuchen, diese Musik zu verstehen. Ich fuhr nach Paris, um den Cembalobauer Marc Ducornet aufzusuchen und kaufte bei ihm einen kleinen Bausatz, den ich mit einem Freund zusammensetze. Ich baute fünf, sechs, sieben Cembali, die ich später wieder verkaufte. Ich wollte versuchen zu verstehen, warum das so funktionierte. Dieses Konzert war ein Auslöser. Ich stellte die Verbindung zur geistlichen Musik her, die ich als Organist des Kirchenchors gespielt hatte, und begann, meine Nase ein wenig in Schallplatten zu stecken.

Heute ist es ein ganz komisches Gefühl für mich, wieder Cembalo zu spielen. Das tat ich kürzlich in Brügge, um für den Continuospieler von *Don Quichotte chez la Duchesse* einzuspringen. Ich fühlte mich vierzig Jahre zurückversetzt! Es amüsierte mich ebenso wie die Musiker. Aber ich tue es nicht mehr. Es gibt Leute, die das tausendmal besser machen als ich."

TANZ

„Ursprünglich ging ich nach Paris, weil ich Tänzer werden wollte. Ich hatte dafür etwas Talent: Ich konnte gut springen, mich gut drehen, ich war gelenkig. Ich hatte in Abbeville begonnen, am Konservatorium von Amiens weitergemacht, drei Monate am Konservatorium von Paris verbracht und dann war's plötzlich aus. Die Idee den Beruf mit vierzig Jahren beenden zu müssen, weil man alt wird, fand ich deprimierend. Und Tänzer ist man außerdem rund um die Uhr. Man muss sich die ganze Zeit, das ganze Leben lang um seinen Körper und seine Gelenkigkeit kümmern. Ich las leidenschaftlich gern, bildete mich gern weiter, forschte gern, und was ich mit meiner Klavierlehrerin flüchtig gestreift hatte – die Handschriften – begann mich zu jucken. Also ließ ich das Tanzen sein, und das war sehr gut für den Tanz! Um meine Unterrichtsstunden zu bezahlen, begleitete ich andere Tanz-stunden. Noëlla Pontois, vor vierzig Jahren Primaballerina an der Oper von Paris, hatte mich in einem Kurs in Paris bemerkt und mir vorgeschlagen, manchmal den Klavierbegleiter zu vertreten. Wie es sich so ergab – aber auch nach einer Aufnah-meprüfung – kam ich als Pianist für das Ballett an die Pariser Oper. Anschließend arbeitete ich ein wenig mit dem Chor und für die Bühne; so habe ich mir dort eine Stellung erarbeitet.

Ich lernte den Anforderungen der Pariser Oper nachzukommen. Vom Studium bin ich zu einem Beruf mit den besten Choreographen der Welt, den besten Tänzern der Welt übergegangen. Mit Nurejew als Chef! Ich hatte keine Zeit mich anzu-passen, doch die schreckliche, rasend schnelle Ausbildung prägte mich. Diese Periode bleibt eine *extrem* wichtige Zeit in meinem Leben.

Heute ist der Tanz für mich nützlich, um beim Dirigieren nicht zu enge Gesten zu machen. Ich bin recht beweglich, habe lange Arme und keine Angst, sie zu öffnen. Ich bewege mich, gehe, ja. Und dann hat auch Vieles in der Musik mit dem Tanz zu tun. Meine musikalischen Lösungen habe ich oft dem Tanz zu verdanken. Und beim Begleiten ist er mir besonders nützlich."

BNF

„Es war in den 1970er Jahren, mitten in den An-fängen des neu erwachten Interesses am Barock mit Christopher Hogwook, Gustav Leonhardt und Jean-Claude Malgoire, René Jacobs und Philippe Herreweghe. Ich war Gasthörer bei William Christie. Der Unterricht fand in klei-nen Räumen des Konservatoriums für einen sehr begrenzten Kreis statt: In einem Gang, ganz hinten in einem Ballettsaal oder in einem Halbgeschoss wurde ein Cembalo aufgestellt, man stand um das Instrument herum und las Kantaten und alte „Dinger" vom Blatt. William Christie erhielt später seine eigene Klasse. Er war unumgänglich – hochgelehrt, seiner so sicher, hatte er *alles* gelesen!

Selbstverständlich war ich nicht nur fasziniert, weil er auf alles eine Antwort wusste, sondern auch weil er im Gegensatz zu den Dirigenten, die ich an der Oper sah, von Rhetorik, Figuralismus, Geschichte, Musikwissenschaft, Instrumenten-kunde, wissenschaftlicher Forschung, Autografen und Handschriften sprach! Ich kam aus meiner Provinz, wo der einzige Bestand an Musikalien der des Pfarrers und der Nonnen der Schule war, während ich in Paris für 7 Francs einen Passierschein der französischen Nationalbibliothek bekommen konnte und zu den Manuskripten von Campra und vielen anderen Zugang hatte! Ich erinnere mich noch an den ersten Kontakt mit dem Stuhl im Lesesaal des fünften Stocks, ich konnte es nicht fassen! Ich war zwanzig Jahre alt und ging jede Woche ganze Tage lang hin. Eine richtige Sucht!

William Christie und Nikolaus Harnoncourt – deren Konzerte ich mir anhörte – hatten Antworten, weil sie nicht *gelernt* sondern *geforscht* hatten. Sie gehörten in dieser Zeit zu den einzigen, die wussten, was sie wussten, weil sie selbst Forschung betrieben hatten. Und wenn sie keine Zeit für die Forschung hatten, schickten sie uns, um für sie zu forschen. Daher kommt meine Freude an dieser ständigen Schatzsuche."

VÖLLIG VERRÜCKT

Vor vierzig Jahren war der Großteil des alten Repertoires noch unentdeckt. Aber auch heute gibt es völlig verrückte, vor Leidenschaft glühende Musikwissenschaftler der Grundlagenforschung, die Lösungen finden, die man vor dreißig, zwanzig, ja sogar zehn Jahren nicht kannte. Und es gibt junge Ensembles, die Repertoire suchen und andere Verhaltensweisen annehmen – weil man in diesem Bereich immer natürlicher wird. Wie erfrischend!

Zugegeben, wir haben das Glück, als künstlerischen Leiter des Centre de musique baroque de Versailles einen königlichen Narren und hochgebildeten Mann zu haben, nämlich Benoît Dratwicki. Ohne ihn wären noch viele Gebiete des französischen Repertoires unbeachtet geblieben.

Dreißig Jahre nach der Gründung des Concert Spirituel nehme ich weiterhin das Risiko auf mich, unbekannte Werke in meine Programme aufzunehmen. Früher ging ich dabei unsystematisch vor, weil ich auf alles Appetit hatte. Aber mit fortschreitendem Alter muss man seine Energie kanalisieren; ich gehe mehr und mehr auf meine Geschmacksrichtungen ein. Wenn ich Benevolo spiele, folge ich meinem Hang für die unbekannte italienische Polyphonie; mache ich viel aus dem 19.-20. Jh., dann in Erinnerung an meine Jahre an der Pariser Oper. Mit dem Palazzetto Bru Zane und dem Centre de musique baroque de Versailles habe ich zwei sehr solide, mit Forschern gespickte Institutionen an meiner Seite, die mir ein Repertoire nach meinem Geschmack verschaffen, weil sie mich kennen."

KOFFER

„Mein Job besteht darin, ein Werk zu verstehen, eine Vorstellung davon zu haben und über Fachkräfte zu verfügen – die Musiker –, die meine Ideen umsetzen können. Ich muss auf die Proben mit Koffern voller Dinge kommen, die ich weitergeben möchte – sei es im Concert Spiruel, im Brussels Philharmonic, in Lissabon oder in Budapest. Jedes Projekt ist *wirklich* wichtig und verdient all die geleistete Arbeit. Ein Musiker hat nicht fünfzehn Jahre studiert, in seiner Jugend keinen Sport getrieben, stundenlang Tonleitern geübt und an Wettbewerben teilgenommen, um sich dann als Berufsmusiker im Leben anzuöden! Er langweilt sich, wenn der Dirigent seiner Aufgabe nicht gewachsen ist, sei es kulturell, sozial, menschlich oder musikalisch. Sobald man aber die Werkzeugkiste öffnet, um über Musikwissenschaft, Verständnis oder Rhetorik zu sprechen, sind sie glücklich! Wenn jemand etwas *bringt* - und sei es Widerspruch, Unerwartetes, Ergebnis einer Forschung, eines Gedankens – ist die Debatte offen, und das verschafft dem Leben eines Musikers zwangsläufig ein anderes Licht. Wenn ich von „Leben" spreche, handelt es sich wirklich um ihr Leben, denn die Musiker beschäftigen sich sechs oder zehn Stunden pro Tag mit ihrem Instrument und der Musik. Ein Dirigent darf das Engagement, die Arbeit und die Energie, die dafür erforderlich sind, gar nicht unterschätzen. Ein Orchester ist kein Werkzeug: Es sind Menschen."

KARRIERE

„Auf meine Karriere bin ich nicht besonders stolz. Ich bin eher glücklich als stolz. Wenn ich das Gebäude in der Rue de Madrid betrete, in dem sich das Pariser Konservatorium befand, als ich zwanzig Jahre alt war, empfinde ich heute noch etwas Schmerzliches. Während meiner Zeit an der Pariser Oper, gab es zahlreiche Beziehungen zwischen den Musikern der Oper, den Korrepetitoren der Oper und den Professoren des Konservatoriums. Man bat mich also, Prüfungsaufgaben für die Studenten des Konservatoriums zu schreiben, für die Aufnahmeprüfung, die Prüfungen im Vom-Blatt-Spielen, die Variationen usw., dabei war ich nie aufgenommen worden! Dieser Komplex veranlasst mich nicht dazu, etwas *beweisen* zu wollen, aber zu *erforschen*. Ich finde mich nie gebildet genug und das ermuntert mich, mich an die Arbeit zu machen."

TRUPPE

„An der Pariser Oper lernte ich, in einem Haus zu leben, zur Truppe zu gehören. Wenn ich in ein Opernhaus komme, kenne ich daher rasch alle – den Inspizienten, den Requisiteur, die Kostümbildnerin, die Chefgarderobierin, den Schnürbodentechniker, den Beleuchter und die Vornamen von allen ... Es geht so viel schneller, ist effizienter, angenehmer und einfacher, wenn man sich danach an die richtige Person mit ihrem Vornamen wendet! Es gibt so viele Leute hinter der Bühne, die ihr Leben immer im Dunkel des Theaters verbringen, nie gewürdigt werden – und dennoch sind es Künstler, die es uns ermöglichen, im Licht zu stehen. *Jeder* ist wichtig. *Jede Funktion* ist wichtig! Und da entsteht Harmonie, und wenn es harmonisch ist, gibt es Gerechtigkeit, Rhythmus und alles, was nötig ist, um das, was in der Partitur steht, zum Leben zu erwecken. Wenn Harmonie herrscht, ist alles vorhanden – aber dafür muss jeder an seinem Platz sein und diesen als wesentlich betrachten."

BRAZZAVILLE

„Wenn man von der Realität abgeschnitten ist, wenn ein Künstler nicht mit dem Leben verbunden ist, ist er ein Faulpelz! Ich war oft in Afrika, besonders im Kongo unter Mobutu: Ich hatte Freundschaft mit den Menschen geschlossen, die vom Konservatorium von Brazzaville übrigblieben. Mit einer Sängerin und einem Gitarristen – und mit mir am Klavier – arbeiteten und spielten wir vierzehn Tage lang für die Professoren. Sie hatten keinen Bleistift, kein Stück Papier. Jahre hindurch schickte ich ihnen mit Hilfe der Botschaft kiloweise Papier, kiloweise Bleistifte. Und dann kam eines Tages mein Packet zurück: Es gab kein Konservatorium mehr, man hatte sie alle getötet. Diese Menschen wurden getötet, weil sie versucht hatten, eine Kunst zu lernen, die der Idee der herrschenden Diktatur nicht entsprach. Seither ertrage ich es nicht mehr, wenn ein Musiker mir gegenüber bei der Probe oder beim Konzert nicht hundertprozentig konzentriert ist. Ich sehe noch die Gesichter all dieser Freunde vor mir, die wegen der Musik gestorben sind …"

REGISSEURE

„Ich habe sehr gute Erfahrungen mit Regisseuren gemacht, besonders mit Christoph Marthaler, Romeo Castellucci und natürlich mit Shirley und Dino. Alle vier sind äußerst kultiviert und arbeiten enorm viel. Sie üben ihren Beruf in verschiedener Weise aus, aber sie lieben ihre Arbeit. Christoph Marthaler zum Beispiel: In seinem Kopf ist alles bereit, aber er weiß nicht, was er machen wird. Wir verbringen fünf Wochen gemeinsam, wir proben die Oper gemeinsam, wir wissen nicht, wohin uns das führt, aber am Tag der Aufführung funktioniert es. Romeo seinerseits ist ein außerordentlicher Illustrator und Bildkünstler, d.h. dass er einen in sein Geschichtenbuch mitnimmt. Wie in *Alice im Wunderland* traut man seinen Augen nicht. Und Gilles und Corinne kennen Racine, Corneille und Molière in- und auswendig, sie verstehen es, eine Truppe zu leiten, und wenn man kommt, um mit der Arbeit zu beginnen, ist alles bereit. Sehr gern habe ich auch mit Mariame Clément gearbeitet. Sie ist äußerst gut vorbereitet, sehr offen, bringt Poesie in den geringsten Szenenwechsel und achtet auch den geringsten Mitarbeiter.
Nichts ist je einfach, und gibt es Schwierigkeiten, muss man sich damit abfinden. Wenn ich eine Produktion akzeptiert habe, muss ich sie zu Ende führen – außerdem ist man für die Leute verantwortlich, die man engagiert hat. Manchmal macht man Erfahrungen, die nicht genial sind, bei denen einem aber trotzdem etwas gelingt. Eine Opernproduktion zu leiten, heißt auch, viele Sorgen in Angriff zu nehmen. Man muss bereit sein, alle möglichen Situationen zu retten und die Künstler auf der Bühne nicht in Gefahr zu bringen."

SHIRLEY & DINO

„Ich habe den sicheren Instinkt für die Bühne durch Corinne und

Gilles Benizio entdeckt – eigentlich erst vor recht kurzer Zeit -, aber ich habe vor allem entdeckt, dass es sich um einen äußerst schwierigen Beruf handelt. Was für eine Arbeit! Aber wenn sie gemacht ist, ist sie wunderbar! Zuvor nahm ich mich sehr ernst, wenn ich eine Tragödie dirigierte, doch dann sah ich die Schwierigkeit, Komik hervorzurufen!!! In einer Tragödie sind die Kniffe sehr klar. Bei der Komik muss man einen regen Geist haben und vor allem Mathematiker sein, um auf die halbe Sekunde genau zu reagieren. Das Ungefähre funktioniert nicht: Man braucht eine genaue Vorstellung vom Rhythmus und muss den anderen und sich gegenüber anspruchsvoll sein.

Mit Gilles und Corrine teilen wir den gleichen Hang für dieselben Dinge, weil wir derselben Generation angehören. Wir erlebten die Anfänge des Fernsehens, wir bewunderten *La Piste aux étoiles*[1], *Les Branquignols*[2] usw. Wir lachen über das Gleiche und lieben gut verrichtete Arbeit. Wie ich sind sie nicht auf einem Haufen Geld geboren und haben sich auch abgestrampelt um zu erringen, was sie haben. Wir waren immer fähig, mit dreimal nichts zurechtzukommen, und davor fürchten wir uns nicht. Coco kocht leidenschaftlich, ich auch. Gilles isst leidenschaftlich. Ich kenne mich bei Weinen nicht aus, er sehr gut. Er fährt gern Motorrad, ich hasse es. Wir sind enge Freunde geworden und unsere Kinder auch. Doch ursprünglich ist es dazu gekommen, weil wir bei der Arbeit viele Affinitäten hatten."

LE CONCERT SPIRITUEL

„Sein eigenes Unternehmen mit eigener Kraft gründen – wie ich es mit *Le Concert Spirituel* tat – wo jeder Cent wichtig ist, selbst auf die Suche nach den geeigneten Leuten gehen, die Konzerte organisieren, ein Programm zusammenstellen können, selbst mit der Hand die Noten schreiben, weil man über wenig Mittel verfügt – ich habe das gesamte Orchestermaterial der ersten CDs angefertigt, eine kolossale Arbeit –, das bildet den Charakter. Ich kenne den Preis von all dem. Ein Team von Freunden zu gründen, das seit dreißig Jahren funktioniert, ist eine Leistung!

Heute sind wir eine sehr schöne Gemeinschaft, die von selbst harmonisch reagieren kann. Das verdankt sie einer dreißigjährigen Erziehung. Um mit dem *Concert Spirituel* einen Ton hervorzubringen, brauchte ich früher eine ganze Probe, jetzt zehn Minuten. Wenn neue Musiker hinzukommen, kümmern sich die Kollegen um sie, um sie rasch einzugliedern. Ich finde das sehr schön. Und im Gegensatz zu bestimmten Ensembles, die die Neuen an die Pulte ganz hinten setzen oder an wenig heikle Posten, rücken wir sie in den Vordergrund, neben die erste Violine. Sie sind nicht hier, um die Reihen zu füllen! Das ist ziemlich aufwertend für sie, und für uns lohnt sich dieses Risiko fast immer. Das ist wirklich erfreulich!"

---

1 Französische Fernsehsendung von Gilles Margaritis (1964-1978), in der eine Zirkusvorstellung zu sehen war. (Anm. d. Ü.)
2 Beliebte französische Theatertruppe (zwischen den 40er und Anfang der 70er Jahre) (Anm. d. Ü.)

SCHUTZENGEL

Sie glaubten an mich und an meine verrücktesten Projekte – allem zum Trotz! Ohne sie wäre ich nicht, wo ich bin: Jean und Nicole Bru natürlich, die wichtigste Begegnung meines Lebens! Mit Le Concert Spirituel und der Stiftung Bru, die den Palazzetto Bru Zane – Zentrum für romantische französische Musik in Venedig gründete, rettete Nicole Bru mehr als drei Jahrhunderte der französischen Musik. Das verdient mehr als eine Medaille, ich weiß nicht was, vielleicht einen für sie reservierten Platz im Pantheon? Martine Tridde und die Stiftung BNP Paribas waren auch jahrelang wunderbare Partner in Kanada und dann mit dem Concert Spirituel! Jetzt habe ich das riesige Glück vom Mécénat Musical Société Générale, einem großen Mäzen des Concert Spirituel unterstützt zu werden, aber auch von der SMA Gruppe. Das ist nicht erstaunlich, denn die kulturellen Entscheidungsträger dieser Gesellschaften sind sehr kultiviert, musikbegeistert, neugierig, visionär und einige davon sind auch diskrete, leidenschaftliche Amateurmusiker. Auch das Kultusministerium und die Stadt Paris unterstützen treu unser musikalisches Abenteuer.

GELD

„Im Bereich der Musik muss man immer auf Geldsuche sein. Zwei Dinge gehen Hand in Hand, für die ich diesen Beruf ausübe: *erstens* essen und *zweitens* Menschen begegnen. Allein beim Concert Spirituel gebe ich je nach Jahr zweihundert bis zweihundertfünfzig Personen pro Jahr Arbeit. Wenn man im Durchschnitt eine Familie pro Angestellten zählt, kommt man auf tausend Personen. Würde ich das Ensemble auflösen, wären diese Leute in Schwierigkeiten. Wenn man nicht ans Geld denkt, das hereinkommt und an das, das ausgegeben wird, existiert man nicht mehr. Ein Euro ist wirklich ein Euro. Jedes Mal wenn ich auftrete, wird eine Geldsumme ausgegeben. Also darf man sich nicht irren: Man muss die Partituren lesen und sich des Projekts sicher sein. Man wird kein Werk szenisch aufführen, bei dem man das Risiko eingeht, dass alles mit Haut und Haar untergeht.
Der Künstler im Elfenbeinturm ist ein Märchen. Oder aber er ist sagenhaft reich – das gibt es, doch kennt man das Ergebnis. Nein, ich bin für das Leben anderer verantwortlich. Jeder muss gut und einsatzbereit sein, denn sonst wird die Darbietung nicht gut. Um auf das *Zweitens* zurückzukommen, ist die Musik nur ein Alibi, um Menschen zu begegnen. Ich merke, dass wir alle, die Musiker und ich, am meisten Vergnügen während der Proben haben. Ein gutes Konzert zu geben, wobei es gelingt, alles was man bei den Proben an Detailverständnis gehortet hat wiederzugeben, ist das Tüpfelchen auf dem i.“

LUXUSHOTEL

„Ein Konzert mit einem Dirigenten ohne Musiker ist nichts. Das gibt es nicht! Ich muss dafür sorgen, dass jeder Musiker oder Sänger seinen richtigen Platz einnimmt. Denn erst in diesem Austausch geschieht etwas. *Le Concert Spirituel* bringt als Barockensemble einen Klang hervor, der keinem der anderen, mir bekannten Orchester gleicht. Wir haben eine solide Basis, Klangfülle, Virtuosität, Liebe fürs Detail, weil *alle* Mitarbeiter wichtig sind. Dafür ist tägliche Arbeit vonnöten: Kein einziger hat das Recht sich zu setzen, wenn er nicht hundertprozentig effizient ist, weil ich das spüre, ich das brauche. Und eben dadurch fühlt jeder, dass er wirklich wichtig ist – also wird er gut. Tatsächlich stellen wir hohe Ansprüche an uns: Wir haben keine Zeit zu verlieren und wir verlieren keine Zeit.

Das entspricht der Verwaltung eines „Hauses". Ich bin von Luxushotels fasziniert. Und der Geist eines Luxushotels erfordert, dass alles geregelt, dass der Kunde wichtig ist und dass sich *alle von allem* betroffen fühlen. Ich bekenne mich zum Concert Spirituel wie zu einem Haus, in dem jeder seinen Platz hat und in dem somit jeder *verantwortlich* ist."

PERSÖNLICHKEITEN

„Im Bereich der Musik geschieht nichts ohne Begegnungen. Und es gibt wunderbare Persönlichkeiten! Was wäre Le Concert Spirituel ohne den lautstarken René Koering, den leidenschaftlichen Benoît Dratwicki, den kultivierten Michel Franck, den aus der Reihe tanzenden Laurent Brunner, die herausragende Michèle Paradon, den anspruchsvollen Emmanuel Hondré und all die unermüdlichen Direktoren der Festivals in ganz Frankreich, die ihrer Region – egal ob sie klein oder groß ist – Ausstrahlung verleihen, wie etwa René Martin mit seiner *Folle Journée*? Von all jenen Tendenzen ganz zu schweigen, denen es gelingt, Veranstalter auf der ganzen Welt zu überzeugen, Boismortier, Bouteiller, Le Prince oder Benevolo aufs Programm zu setzen, und das von Mexiko bis Peking, von Seoul bis Varaždin, von Warschau bis Istanbul!"

LACHEN

„Was ich mit den Tänzern lachen konnte, als ich an der Oper von Paris war! Aber ich lachte, weil es für alle sehr hart war. Lachen ist ein wunderbares Ventil, und die Tänzer sind wirklich sehr witzig. Viele Leute kritisieren mich, weil ich das Profil eines Dirigenten profaniere, wenn ich herumalbere. Bei einem Piloten einer Boeing 747 würde ich das verstehen, aber bei einem Dirigenten? Kein Beinbruch! Wenn ich herumalbere, arbeite ich gründlich. Und auch wenn ich herumalbere, verliere ich deshalb nicht meine Fähigkeiten der Analyse, des Zuhörens und der Entschlusskraft. Meine Anforderungen sind die gleichen.

Aber Achtung: Auch wenn ich den Anschein gebe, mich auf der Bühne zu amüsieren, ist das nur ein Eindruck. Ich *sterbe* vor Lampenfieber! Man sieht es vielleicht nicht, weil ich ein Profi bin. Ich gebe meinen Stress nicht an alle weiter, wo ich doch dafür bezahlt werde, den Stress aller im Griff zu haben!

Lachen setze ich bei den Proben oft ein. So werden die musikalischen und technischen Informationen durch Humor aufgelockert, was zwei Auswirkungen hat: alle zu entspannen, wenn sie sehr konzentriert sind – man kann sich nicht drei Stunden lang konzentrieren –, und den Klang zu ändern – wenn man entspannt ist, liegt der Schwerpunkt sehr tief und man hat viele Grundtöne. Wenn man hie und da lacht, atmen die Musiker besser, die Ohren öffnen sich und man macht rasch Fortschritte. Nichts als Vorteile!"

STIMMEN

„Le Concert Spirituel hätte ohne Stimmen, ohne Chor nicht bestehen können. Man darf nicht vergessen, dass das dem ästhetischen Ideal der Barockzeit entspricht, die versucht, die Natur nachzuahmen. Aber was ist die Natur? Die Stimme. Ich wäre enttäuscht, wenn Le Concert Spirituel nur ein Orchester wäre.

Dagegen hätten wir uns auf die geistliche Musik beschränken können, das schon, weil die große Motette eine Art französische Oper ist, aber ohne Ärger mit der Inszenierung, den Bühnenbildern und den Kostümen: Man ist sein eigener Regisseur. Opern führt man mit demselben Diskurs, demselben Orchester, demselben Chor und derselben Anzahl an Solisten auf. Die Sprache ist *genau* die gleiche! In einer Motette gibt es Stürme, Erdbeben, leidenschaftliche Liebe, Septakkorde – wie in der Oper. Manchmal sogar besser, weil man demonstrativer sein muss, um das Fehlen der visuellen Seite auszugleichen.

Was mich bei einer Stimme ergreift? Alles! Für den Chor suche ich nicht unbedingt hübsche Stimmen, sondern eine Zusammensetzung der Stimmen, die ja nicht alle gleich sein sollen. Wenn man ein gutes Pult zusammenstellen möchte, ist eine ganze Skala verschiedener Klangfarben nötig. So vervielfacht man seine Ausdruckspalette. Für den Chor suche ich also keinesfalls ein einheitliches Stimmmodell. Das macht Le Concert Spirituel erkennbar, u.zw. an der Palette seiner Klangfarben, an einer gewissen Dreistigkeit.

Bei den Solisten hängt es von der Rolle und dem Werk ab. Ich arbeite gern mit jemandem, mit dem ich mich wohlfühle und der nicht auf seinen Positionen, seiner Stimme, seinen hohen oder tiefen Tönen, seiner Atmung, seiner Partitur besteht … der zum Beispiel akzeptiert, sich schwach zu geben, wenn die Rolle das erfordert.

FAULPELZ

„Im Grunde meines Herzens bin ich ein Faulpelz. Das hat vielleicht meinen Hang zum Analysieren entwickelt, um effizienter zu sein und mit meiner Energie zu sparen. Und außerdem beobachte ich gern – und ich hatte Posten, wo ich das tun konnte. Was mich weiterhin vorwärtsbringt, ist eine Reihe verschiedener Dinge: Ich wurde nicht zum Dirigenten erzogen, ich erlernte das Dirigieren erst nach dem klassischen Studium und nur ziemlich kurz. Ich wurde sofort an die Pariser Oper engagiert, wo ich analysieren konnte, was man mir aus dem Berufsleben erzählte. Ich hatte keinen klassischen Studiengang fürs Dirigieren gemacht.

Ich hatte das Glück, acht Jahre lang an der Pariser Oper zu arbeiten und dort so ziemlich alle Posten innezuhaben – acht Jahre, nach denen ich genug davon hatte, keine *musikalischen Entscheidungen* treffen zu können; ich wollte mich ein bisschen mehr um mich kümmern. Als Pianist war ich auf der Seite der Interpreten, ich konnte also sehen, was man von einem Dirigenten *hinnehmen* muss. Sänger war ich auch, so konnte ich sehen, was man von einem Chef *nicht hinnehmen wollte*. Ich lerne oft durch das Negative: Es ist sehr wichtig zu wissen, was man nicht nachmachen möchte, weil man darunter gelitten hat. Das ist nicht schwierig: Man muss es nur *analysieren* – aber dieses Phänomen vergisst man oft."

BOISMORTIER

„Boismortier ist wirklich ein Genie! Ganz einfach, nicht angeberisch, nicht belehrend wie Rameau. Jedes Mal wenn man seine Musik hört, wird es Sonntag Vormittag, es riecht nach Croissants, es ist schön, und der Hund kommt, um sich streicheln zu lassen. Das ist Boismortier. Zehn Jahre lang verglich ich die Themen, die Rameau und Boismortier gemein sind, ihre orchestralen Erfindungen: Boismortier erringt immer den ersten Platz. Er wird sehr wenig gespielt, weil er wie Poulenc Dilettant ist. Er ist so genial, dass das, was er schreibt, vollkommen ist, aber da er Geld verdient, ist er allen ein Dorn im Auge, allen voran Herrn Rameau. Physiologisch gesehen, ist es absolut wunderbar, seine Musik zu spielen: Sie ist organisch – für alle Instrumente, für die er schrieb. Mit jedem Takt erzeugt man Glück! Selbst die geringste Flötensonate ist großartig. Er ist wirklich mein Lieblingskomponist."

FRANZÖSISCHE MUSIK

„Es gibt ein Konzept der Einheit des Kulturerbes. Musik ist nicht um der Musik willen da: Sie ist ein Teil jener französischen Kultur, in der ich mich wohlfühle; ich trenne sie nicht von der impressionistischen Malerei oder der Geschichte des Tanzes oder der Literatur, die ich liebe, der Architektur, dem Mobiliar, den Kostümen usw. Als ich mit Serge Lifar arbeitete, hatte ich das Gefühl, in direkter Verbindung mit der Geschichte zu stehen, die von Lully ausging. Das Vergnügen, französische Musik zu spielen, heute noch Partituren zu entdecken, ist gleich geblieben. Ich fühle mich dabei sehr wohl: Ich fühle mich beim Erklären davon sehr wohl, weil ich die Schlüssel dazu habe, und zwar nicht nur die musikalischen. Ich kann ein neues Licht darauf werfen, das mir für jede Musik dient, an die ich herangehe, sei sie barock oder nicht. Ohne den rhetorischen Rahmen, den Symbolismus, existiert nichts. Ich komme aus dieser Kultur und habe das alte Repertoire studiert, was mir erlaubt, an alles mit dem gleichen semiotischen Raster heranzugehen. All die Entdeckungen, die vor einigen Jahrzehnten über die Barockmusik gemacht wurden, veränderten die Interpretation dieser Musik aber auch die Interpretation der gesamten darauffolgenden Musik."

SPRACHE

„Was mich an der französischen Musik ergreift? Ganz einfach: die Sprache. Sie ist meine Muttersprache – welch unglaublicher Reichtum ist es doch, eine Sprache zu beherrschen. Und Lully benutzt die gleiche wie Poulenc, die Arbeit ist daher die gleiche: Es gibt prosodische Akzente, Liaisons, I- und A- und U-Laute. Wenn man den Text ohne Interpretation spricht, ist der Rhythmus bereits da. Der Komponist baut seinen Rhythmus darauf auf. Dann kommen die Tonhöhen dazu mit den Modulationen des Textes und das Ganze ist geritzt!

Ich mache nicht Musik: Ich mache Worte. Wenn man die Worte nicht versteht, versteht man die Poesie nicht; wenn man die Poesie nicht versteht, versteht man die Handlung nicht und weiß nicht, warum man hier ist! In der Zeit Lullys interessierte es niemanden, etwas zu hören, was man nicht verstand. Man sah sich *Armide* von Monsieur Quinault auf eine Musik von Lully an – also vor allem einen Text. Und Rameau sagte, dass er es vorzieht, unter seinen Interpreten eine Schauspielerin zu haben, die eine recht schöne Stimme hat, als eine Sängerin.

Darin besteht das Wesen der Oper: in der Vertonung eines Textes. Man braucht die Musik an sich nicht, sie ist nur eine begleitende Geste, um *gut* zu sprechen. Als Ausgangspunkt ist eine verständliche, intelligente Stimme vonnöten. Wir machen keine Stimmungsmusik. Man muss sich um die Worte kümmern, die Energie darauf richten, die Worte zu verstehen. Die Komponisten sind so gebildet, sie kennen die Physiologie des Gesanges so gut, dass sie ihre Musik auf der Grundlage der Muskeln aufbauen, um effizient zu sein. Also vertrauen Sie den Worten! Das sage ich den Solisten, die oft ihre Interpretation in den Vordergrund rücken, anstatt zu beobachten und ihre Technik ohne Leidenschaft einzusetzen. Ergebnis: Sie überdosieren, und man versteht nichts. Wenn sie sich bewusst werden, dass sie mit dreimal weniger Energie verständlicher sind, haben sie es geschafft. Es ist eine große physiologische Hilfe, ein sehr einfaches Mittel, die Zuhörer zu überzeugen; wenn die Sänger das erst einmal verstanden haben, bedienen sie sich dessen mit Genuss. Im Klang des Textes liegt ein echtes Glücksgefühl: Man spürt, dass sich alles öffnet, man hat eine Hörweite, eine Stimmprojektion, man ist mit dem Werk verbunden, alles ist logisch."

PRIX DE ROME

(ROMPREIS) „Wer nahm am *Prix de Rome* teil, um einen Aufenthalt in der Villa Medici zu erhalten? Die Schüler des Pariser Konservatoriums, also die Elite der Schüler. Unter dieser Elite der jeweiligen Klasse wählten die Professoren, die ihrerseits große Stars waren, ihre besten Schüler. Also die Elite der Elite. Und diese Elite der Elite trat beim Wettbewerb um den *Prix de Rome* an, also die Elite der Elite der Elite. Und die Elite der Elite der Elite der Elite erhielt einen Aufenthalt in der Villa Medici. Also waren die Gewinner zwangsweise alle sehr gut, sie konnten alle komponieren. Gemeinsam mit dem Palazzetto Bru Zane hatten wir die Idee, alle Preisträger des *Prix de Rome* aufzunehmen – dreihundert erste Preise und sechshundert zweite –, was Aufnahmen verhieß, die einige Jahre dauern sollten. Davon gingen wir aus. Und dann suchten wir nach den Familien dieser Komponisten. Die Musiker konnten es nicht fassen: Sie spielen Musik aus dem 19. Jh. und die Familie des Komponisten kommt, um der Probe zuzuhören! Sie hatten aus den Augen verloren, dass die Musik von richtigen Menschen geschrieben wird und nicht von Verlagshäusern. Als Patrice d'Ollone kam und die Wettbewerbsstücke seines Großvaters hörte, die dieser nie gehört hatte, weinte er vier Tage lang. Das war nichts Abstraktes, das war Max, sein Großvater! Das ändert alles und es änderte den Klang des Orchesters. Und das interessiert mich.

Also: der *Prix de Rome* und dann unmögliche Dinge, die andere nicht machen wollen, Dinge, die undurchführbar scheinen, weil es sich um aussichtslose Heldentaten handelt. Mit Alexandre Dratwicki wollten wir zunächst das Publikum nicht erschrecken, daher wählten wir bekannte Namen: Debussy, dann Saint-Saëns, Charpentier, Max d'Ollone – eine Offenbarung! – , Dukas – absolut überwältigend! –, Gounod usw. Die Partituren von Dukas fanden wir zufällig in einem Karton im Konservatorium, alle Werke, die er nicht verbrannt hatte – er verbrannte zwei Drittel seiner Kompositionen. Alles, was er aus Rom geschickt hatte, seine Kantaten, Meisterwerke! *Polyeucte* – Dukas war zweiundzwanzig oder dreiundzwanzig Jahre alt, es war noch vor 1900 ... Hollywood hat ihm alles gestohlen! Ein Genie! So trafen wir unsere Wahl. Wir konnten uns nicht vorstellen, mit Komponisten wie Véronge de la Nux oder Deffés zu beginnen.

Für diese wirklich großen Meisterwerke begeistere ich mich doppelt: Weil die andern denken, dass es sich um Werke unbedeutender junger Komponisten handelt. Und weil ich das einfach mag.

Das Projekt mit dem Palazzetto Bru Zane beenden wir 1920. Weiter gehe ich auf keinen Fall. Messiaen oder Dutilleux kannte ich, und dafür gibt es andere, die das besser machen als ich."

CD

„Ich mache viele Aufnahmen. Ich arbeite nämlich auf einem Gebiet – der alten Musik – wo man viel entdeckt, viel liest, viel produziert. Man *muss* hier viel hinterlassen – wirklich. Man muss Spuren hinterlassen, ohne die man umsonst gearbeitet hätte. Wenn ich sehe, dass die Generation, die heute zwanzig/dreißig Jahre alt ist, bestimmte „große Musiker" nicht kennt, bestätigt das mein Gefühl, dass man etwa hinterlassen muss, da sonst alles verschwindet. Ich hinterlasse Werke, die niemand geahnt hat und um die sich niemand kümmert, wenn wir es mit dem Concert Spiruel nicht tun.

Schließt man sich ein, um eine CD aufzunehmen, ist man von der Welt abgeschnitten und arbeitet absolut an jeder Note. Und man spielt, man spielt nochmals und nochmals. Mit einem Konzert hat das nichts zu tun. Man erzeugt ein Objekt, das einen Moment festhält, den man sich vorstellt, ohne sich von der Stimmung des Tages, den Leuten hinten, dem Luftzug, der aus den Kulissen kommt, usw. beeindrucken zu lassen. Auch die Energie ist ganz anders. Man ist voll engagiert, hier gibt es keine Lässigkeit. Es handelt sich um eine andere Arbeit als die eines Konzerts, wodurch die Qualität der Interpretation verschieden ist. Auch erlaubt man sich bei einer Aufnahme Dinge, die man sich im Konzert nicht erlauben würde und umgekehrt.

Jede CD ist eine Erinnerung – eine Erinnerung an körperliche Anstrengungen – denn sie bedeutet große Arbeit, große Erschöpfung, große Mühe, die man jedoch gern endlos fortsetzen würde. Die CD ist der Höhepunkt der Arbeit, die Arbeit ist vollendet. Zwei CDs haben mich geprägt, wobei eine genau das Gegenteil der anderen ist. Die erste ist die 40stimmige Messe von Striggio: Wir hatten ein verblüffendes Team! Es war ein großer Augenblick nach dreißig Jahren Forschung. Im Gegensatz dazu liebe ich auch die CD der Sonaten für Bassinstrumente von Boismortier mit vier Streicherbässen, zwei Theorben, an den Tasteninstrumenten waren wir zu zweit, und Boismortier war mitten unter uns. Nur Bassinstrumente, der Gipfel des Glücks! Und die CD ist wunderbar. Striggio hätte ohne die mit Boismortier geleistete Arbeit nicht existiert."

SAINT-RIQUIER

„Die Leitung des Kulturzentrums von Saint-Riquier holte mich, ohne auch nur *im geringsten* zu ahnen, dass ich vor fünfundvierzig Jahren Organist in Saint-Riquier war und nur acht Kilometer davon entfernt geboren worden war. Wir begegneten uns in Istanbul. Ich hatte überhaupt nicht beabsichtigt, in diese Gegend zurückzukehren. Ich hatte dort zwar einige Freunde, die ich aber nicht mehr oder selten sah. Und dann sagte ich „ja". Ein einziges Telefongespräch und ich fand vierzig Freiwillige, rief meine alten Freunde an, die ich kenne, seit ich zehn Jahre alt bin. Und ich beschloss, die Programme und Pressemappen ins Pikardische übersetzen zu lassen.

Eine halbe Stunde vor dem großen Konzert, bevor das Publikum eingelassen wurde, schlossen wir die Kirche, um zu sehen, ob alles an seinem Platz ist. Die Leute stellten sich an, und zwei Schauspieler kündeten das Programm auf Pikardisch an. Das erste Mal verwirrte das alle Bourgeois, die aus Lille oder Amiens kamen; und das brachte die Leute aus der Gegend zum Lachen, sie konnten es nicht fassen. Alle begannen mit ihren Nachbarn zu sprechen! Als sie danach sahen, dass wir ein Programm in französischer und pikardischer Sprache verteilten, wurde es richtig laut im Saal. Diejenigen, die nicht Pikardisch verstanden, ließen es sich erklären, und die Pikarden fanden das sehr gut! Es kam zu einem echten Austausch im Publikum. Und heute sammeln die Leute diese Programme, bitten uns um die, die ihnen fehlen, und wir drucken sie nach!"

WEITERGABE DES KNOW-HOWS

„Ich gebe sehr gern Workshops und Meisterklassen, bei denen ich fünfunddreißig bis vierzig Studenten derselben Generation Unterricht gebe; wir verbringen vierzehn Tage miteinander, an denen wir Tag und Nacht an einem Projekt arbeiten. Dann gehen wir auseinander ... und ich finde sie im Berufsleben wieder. Wenn es gelingt, sie in so kurzer Zeit einer Harmonie nahezubringen, ist das äußerst förderlich. Sie werden danach ihr ganzes Leben hindurch auf die Suche nach etwas gehen, das eine Richtlinie für sie sein wird. Ich stelle ihnen viele Fragen, die sie sich nicht stellen. Danach ist es an ihnen, auf die Suche zu gehen, einen Weg einzuschlagen und die Antwort zu finden, und vor allem daraus zu folgern, warum es jedes Mal funktioniert. Sie müssen die Dinge analysieren.

MUSICAL

„In New York, wo ich oft mit der Pariser Oper war, entdeckte ich das Musical und Broadway. In London auch. Ich war davon fasziniert: Da ist Musik, die glücklich macht! Alle Mitwirkenden müssen dabei sehr gut sein, sonst werden sie schon am nächsten Tag ersetzt. Ein Musical zu dirigieren, würde mir sehr Spaß machen; mit *Don Quichotte chez la Duchesse* nähere ich mich diesem Wunsch bereits. Jedenfalls haben *wir* das Musical erfunden, u. zw. mit Lully. Man braucht dazu ein gutes Textbuch, eine gute Geschichte, einen guten Komponisten und vor allem einen guten Bühnenbildner und einen guten Choreographen: Was ist das anderes als ein Musical? Racine und Quinault sagten, sie könnten mit sechzig Wörtern eine Komödie schreiben, und wenn man genau aufpasst, sind es wirklich immer die gleichen Wörter. Die *Tragédie lyrique* ist nun mal so! Man geht hin, um alle szenischen Künste zu sehen! Man ist von einer Maschinerie tiefer beeindruckt als von Lullys Musik.

In dieser Gattung ergreift mich die Musik Michel Legrands tief. Sie ist doch der Höhepunkt der französischen Musik. Er war Schüler von Nadia Boulanger, und wenn er will, kann er eine Beethoven-Symphonie schreiben. Er ist ein Genie, das man unmittelbar erkennen kann, wie Ravel, Beethoven oder Debussy. Unmittelbar!

Meine *Glücksmelodie* bleiben meine Kinder, die sich zanken. Wenn wir beisammen sind, kommt immer ein Augenblick, in dem sie streiten. Ich finde das toll. Sie sind rund um mich, ich existiere absolut nicht mehr! Sie sind erwachsen, sie existieren selbständig, ich bin da, ich störe sie nicht, ich sehe sie an, sie sind schön, dann versöhnen sie sich wieder, und alles beginnt von vorne. Das ist meine Glücksmelodie: meine Kinder.“

Diese Äußerungen wurden am 16. Juni, 29. September und 3. Oktober 2016 von Claire Boisteau gesammelt.

1.

1. Concert à la Cathédrale Saint-Denis avec Véronique Gens 2. Opéra de Paris, séance de travail avec Ninette de Valois, photo prise par Hervé Niquet 3. Saint-Michel-en-Thiérache

2.

1. Haendel, *Fireworks* à la Philharmonie de Paris 2. Boismortier, *Don Quichotte* chez la Duchesse avec Gilles et Corinne Benizio 3. Dans les coulisses de *King Arthur* de Purcell à Versailles (© Raphael Saada) 4. Avec Marie-Geneviève Massé

1.

2.

3.

1. Le Concert Spirituel (© Guy Vivien) 2. Grand Benevolo en 2017 3. En Afrique 4. Le Trio Hervé Niquet à Saint-Denis de la Réunion 5. Le Concert Spirituel à Montpellier 6. Hervé Niquet et ses deux enfants